RAIN A TRIBUTE TO THE BEATLES

ISBN 978-1-61774-240-8

Visit Hal Leonard Online at
www.halleonard.com

ACROSS THE UNIVERSE

Words and Music by JOHN LENNON
and PAUL McCARTNEY

Em7
Gm
3fr
D
sess-ing and ca - ress-ing me.
Jai Gu-ru De - va.
Em7
A7
Om.
Noth-ing's gon - na change my world,
G/D
D
A7
noth-ing's gon-na change my world.
Noth-ing's gon-na change my world,
G/D
D
To Coda
noth-ing's gon-na change my world.

F♯m
Im - ag - es of bro - ken light which dance be - fore me like a mil - lion eyes,
Em7
A
A7
they call me on and on a - cross the u - ni - verse.
D
F♯m
Thoughts me - an - der like a rest - less wind in - side a let - ter - box, they
Em7
A
A7
D.S. al Coda
tum - ble blind - ly as they make their way a - cross the u - ni - verse.

CODA
F♯m
Sounds of laugh - ter, shades of earth are ring - ing through my o-pened ears, in -
Em7
Gm
3fr
D
cit - ing and in - vit - ing me.
Lim - it - less, un - dy - ing love, which
F♯m
Em7
shines a - round me like a mil - lion suns, and calls me on and on a - cross
A
A7
D
the u - ni - verse.
Jai Gu - ru De -

Em7
A7
- va. Om.
Noth-ing's gon-na change my world,
G/D
D
noth-ing's gon-na change my world.
A7
G/D
Noth-ing's gon-na change my world,
noth-ing's gon-na change my world.
D
Repeat and Fade
Optional Ending
Jai Gu-ru De - va.

ALL YOU NEED IS LOVE

Words and Music by JOHN LENNON
and PAUL McCARTNEY

G D/F♯ Em

There's noth - ing you can do that can't be done.
There's noth - ing you can make that can't be made.
There's noth - ing you can know that is - n't known.

G D/F♯ Em

Noth - ing you can sing that can't be sung.
No one you can save that can't be saved.
Noth - ing you can see that is - n't shown.

D7/A G D/F♯ D7/E

Noth-ing you can say but you can learn how to play the game.
Noth-ing you can do but you can learn how to be you in time.
No-where you can be that is - n't where you're meant to be.

It's

D7 D7/C D7 G A7sus

easy. All you need is love,

D7 G A7sus D7

all you need is love.

G B7 Em G/D C D7 To Coda

All you need is love, love. Love is all you need.

G D/F♯ Em G D/F♯

Love, love, love. Love, love,

Em
D/A
G
D7/F♯
D9/E
4fr
D7
D7/C
love.
Love,
love,
love.
D7
G
A7sus
D7
All you need is love,
G
A7sus
D7
G
B7
all you need is love.
All you need is love,
Em
G/D
C
D7
G
D.S. al Coda
love.
Love is all you need.

CODA
G
A7sus
D7
All you need is love.
All to-geth-er now.
G
A7sus
D7
G
B7
All you need is love.
Ev-'ry-bod-y.
All you need is love,
Em
G/D
C
D7
G
D
love.
Love is all you need,
love is all
Repeat and Fade
G
Dsus
Optional Ending
G
you need.
(Love is all you need.)
Love is all
you need.

ALL MY LOVING

Words and Music by JOHN LENNON
and PAUL McCARTNEY

F♯m
B7
E
while I'm a - way,
I'll write home ev - 'ry day
C♯m
A
B7
4fr
and I'll send all my lov - ing to
1
2, 3
E
N.C.
you.
I'll pre -
you.
C♯m
C+
All my lov - ing I will send to

E
C♯m
4fr
you,
all
my
lov - ing,
dar -
C+
To Coda
E
N.C.
- ling,
I'll
be
true.
A
E
F♯m
B7

D.S. al Coda
(Verse1)
(take 2nd ending)
CODA
E
N.C.
Close your
C♯m
4fr
All my lov - ing,
all my
lov - ing,
ooh, all my lov - ing
I will send to you.
3

AND I LOVE HER

Words and Music by JOHN LENNON
and PAUL McCARTNEY

F♯m
C♯m
A
And if you saw my love you'd love her too.
The kiss my lov - er brings she brings to me.
I know this love of mine will nev - er die.
B
E6
To Coda
1
I love her.
And I love her.
And I love her.
2
C♯m
B
A love like ours
C♯m
G♯m
C♯m
could nev - er die as long as I

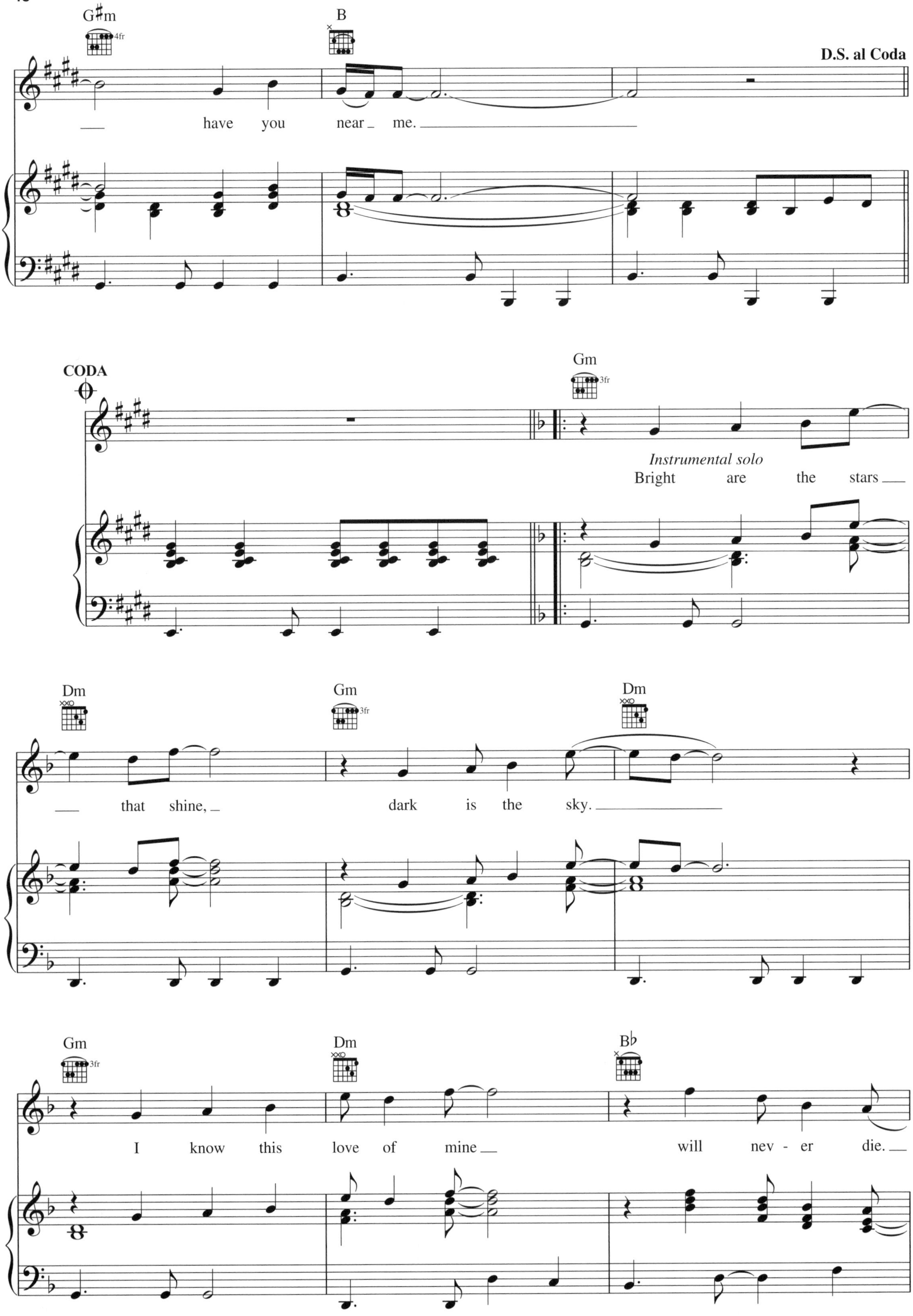
G♯m
4fr
B
D.S. al Coda
have you near me.
CODA
Gm
3fr
Instrumental solo
Bright are the stars
Dm
Gm
3fr
Dm
that shine, dark is the sky.
Gm
3fr
Dm
B♭
I know this love of mine will nev - er die.

C
1
F6
End instrumental solo
And I love
2
F6
her.
Gm
3fr
F6
Gm
3fr
D

BLACKBIRD

Words and Music by JOHN LENNON
and PAUL McCARTNEY

Slowly and smoothly

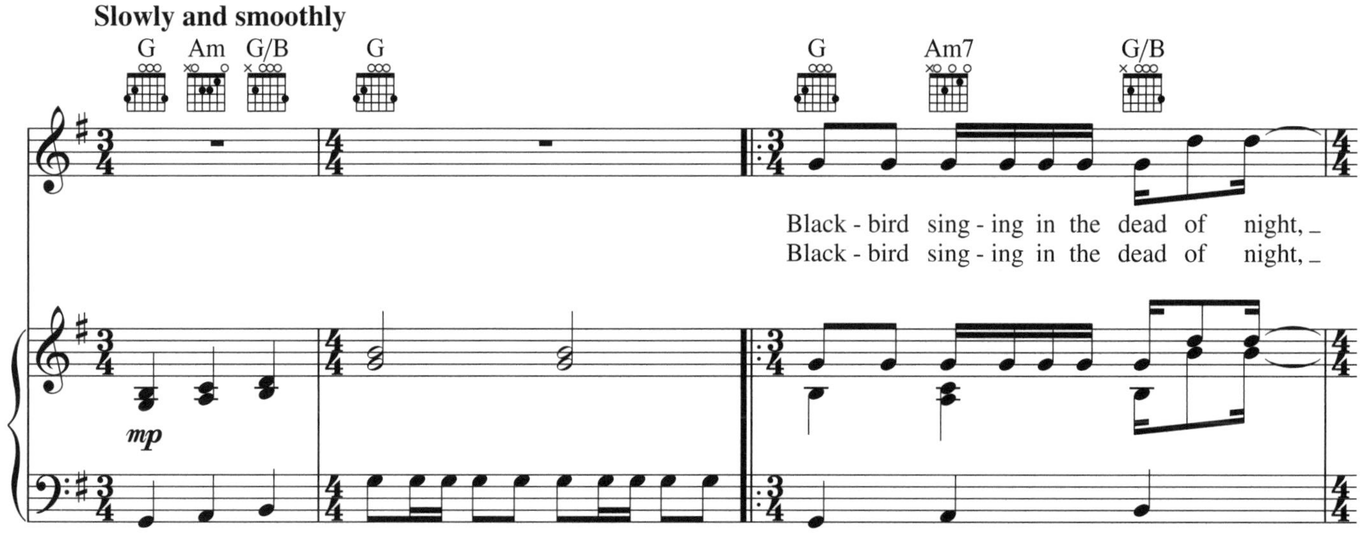

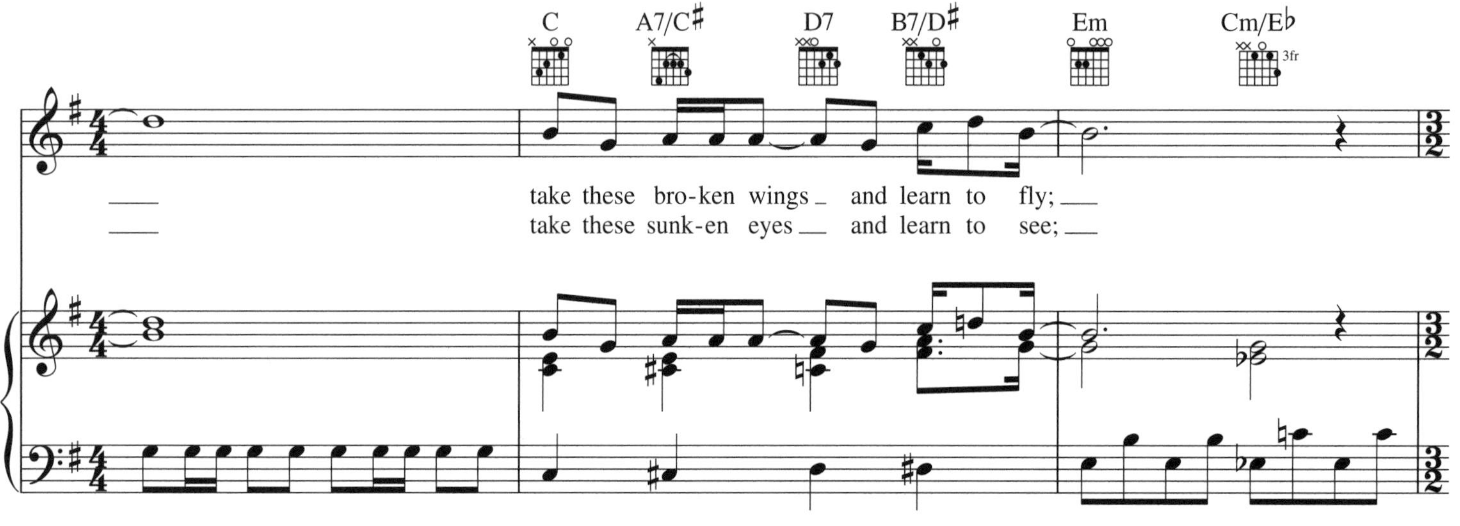

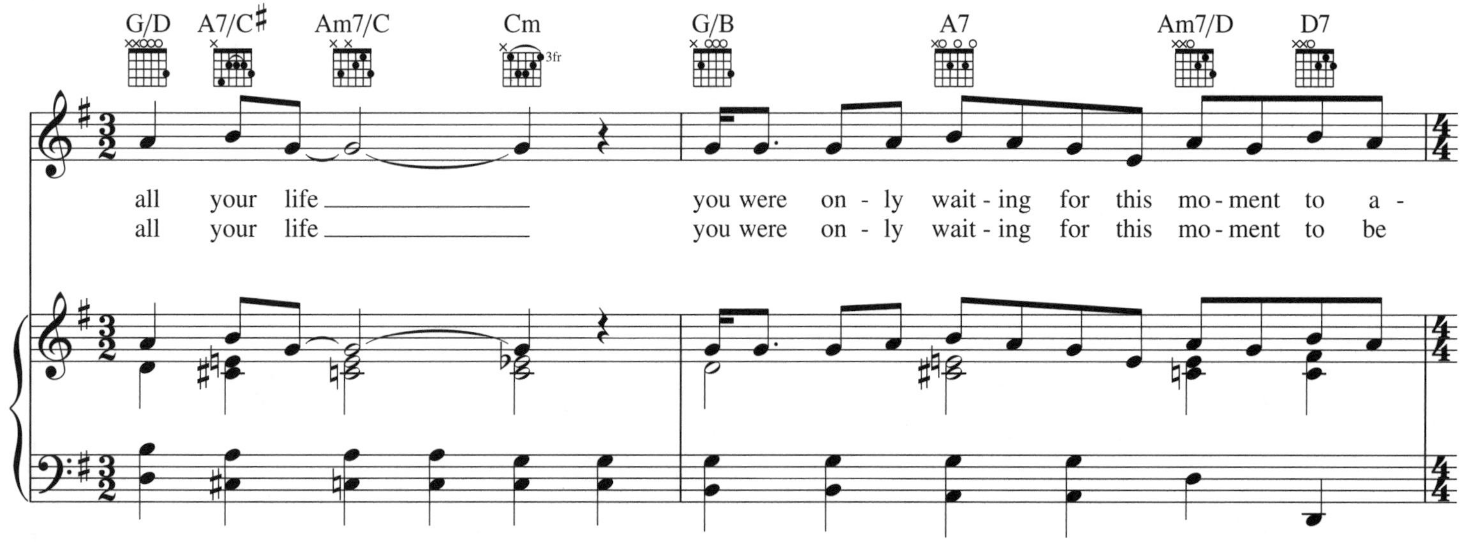

1
G
C
G/B
A7
D7
G
2
G
rise.
free.
F
C/E
Dm
C
B♭
C
F
C/E
Dm
C
Black - bird, fly,
black - bird, fly
B♭
A7
D7
G
Am7
G/B
in - to the light of a dark black night.
G
C
A7/C♯
D7
B7/D♯
Em
Cm/E♭
3fr

Gmaj7/D
A7/C♯
Am7/C
Cm
3fr
G/B
A7
D7
G
F
C/E
Dm
C
B♭
C
F
C/E
Dm
C
Black - bird, fly,
black - bird, fly
B♭
A7
D7
G
Am7
G/B
in - to the light of a dark black night.
G
molto rit.
G
A7
G/B
C
G/B
A7
a tempo

Am7/D G Am7 G/B G
Black-bird sing-ing in the dead of night,
C A7/C♯ D7 B7/D♯ Em Cm/E♭ G/D A7/C♯ Am7/C Cm
3fr
take these bro-ken wings and learn to fly;
all your life
G/B A7 Am7/D D7 G C G/B A7
you were on-ly wait-ing for this moment to a-rise.
You were on-ly wait-ing for this
Am7/D D7 G C G/B A7 Am7/D D7 G
mo-ment to a-rise.
You were on-ly wait-ing for this mo-ment to a-rise.

COME TOGETHER

Words and Music by JOHN LENNON
and PAUL McCARTNEY

Dm7
He wear no shoe - shine, he got toe - jam foot - ball, he got
He Bag Pro - duc - tion, he got wal - rus gum - boot, he got
He roll - er coast - er, he got ear - ly warn - ing, he got
A
mon - key fin - ger, he shoot Co - ca Co - la, he say, "I know you,
O - no side - board, he one spi - nal crack - er, he got feet down be - low
mud - dy wa - ter, he one Mo - jo fil - ter, he say, "One and one and one
G7
N.C.
you know me." One thing I can tell you is you got to be free.
his knee. Hold you in his arm - chair, you can feel his dis - ease.
is three." Got to be good - look - ing 'cause he so hard to see.
Come to - geth -

Bm
Bm/A
G
G/A
3fr
Dm7
- er,
right
now,
o - ver me.
1, 2
3
Repeat and Fade
Come to-geth - er,
Yeah!
Optional Ending
Come to-geth - er,
Yeah!

ELEANOR RIGBY

Words and Music by JOHN LENNON
and PAUL McCARTNEY

Moderately, with a steady beat

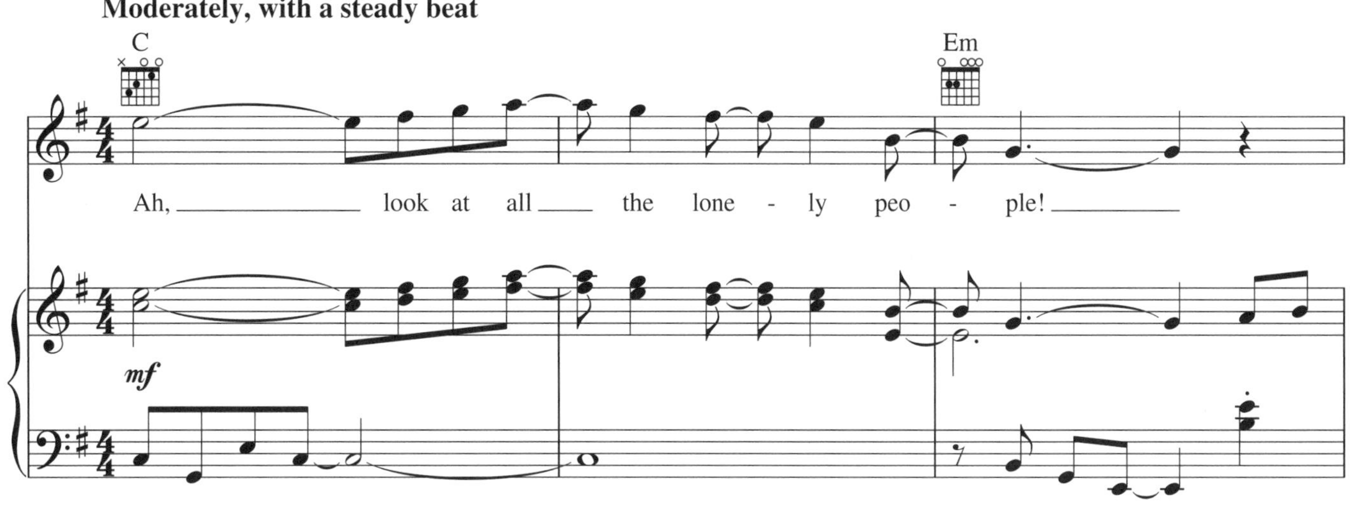

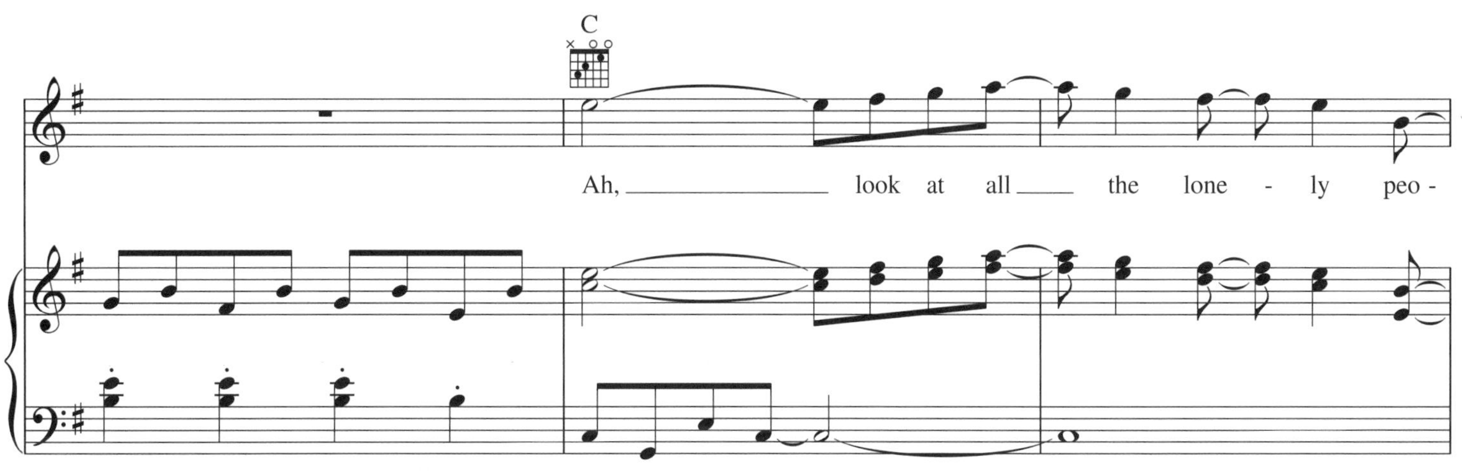

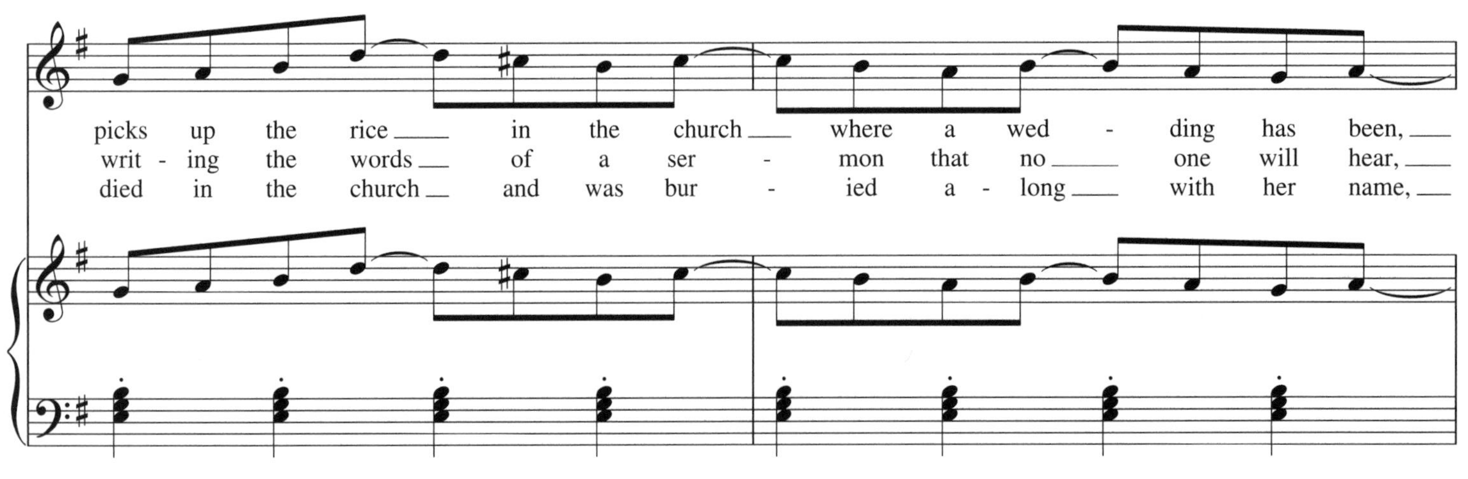
picks up the rice in the church where a wed - ding has been,
writ - ing the words of a ser - mon that no one will hear,
died in the church and was bur - ied a - long with her name,

C
Em
Lives in a dream. Waits at the win - dow,
No one comes near. Look at him work - ing,
No - bod - y came. Fa - ther Mc - Ken - zie,

C
wear - ing the face that she keeps in a jar by the door,
darn - ing his socks in the night when there's no - bod - y there,
wip - ing the dirt from his hands as he walks from the grave,

Em Em7 Em6

who is it for?
what does he care?
no one was saved.
All the lonely people, where do

C/E Em Em7

they all come from?
All the lonely peo-

Em6 C/E To Coda 1 Em

-ple, where do they all be-long?

2 Em D.C. al Coda

CODA Em

A DAY IN THE LIFE

Words and Music by JOHN LENNON
and PAUL McCARTNEY

C
F
Em
Cmaj7
G
Bm/F♯
I saw the pho - to - graph.
He blew his mind out in a
I saw a film to - day, oh
Em
C
Em/B
Am
Cmaj7
car;
he did - n't no - tice that the lights had changed.
boy;
the Eng - lish ar - my had just won the war.
G
Bm
Em
C
F
A crowd of peo - ple stood and stared.
A crowd of peo - ple turned a - way,
They'd seen his face be - fore;
but I just had to look,
1
Em
Em/D
C
no - bod - y was real - ly sure if he was from the House of Lords.

2
Em
Em/D
C
hav - ing read the book.
I'd
Bm/F♯
G
Em/A
love to turn you on.
E
Woke up,
D5
5fr
fell out of bed, dragged a comb a cross my head.
Found my

E
F♯m/B
E
F♯m/B
way down - stairs and drank a cup, and look-ing up, I no-ticed I was late.
E
Found my coat and grabbed my hat made the bus in sec-onds
D5
5fr
E
F♯m/B
B7
flat. Found my way up - stairs and had a smoke. And
E
F♯m/B
C
G
some-bod - y spoke and I went in - to a dream. Ah

D A E

C G D

A E D C D G Bm/F♯

I read the news to - day, oh

Em C Em/B

boy, four thou - sand holes in Black - burn,

Am
Cmaj7
G
Bm
Lan - ca - shire.
And though the holes were rath - er
Em
C
F
small,
they had to count them all;
Em
Em/D
C
now they know how man - y holes it takes to fill the Al - bert Hall.
I'd
Bm/F♯
G
G/A
3fr
E
love to turn you on.

DAY TRIPPER

Words and Music by JOHN LENNON
and PAUL McCARTNEY

A7
tak - ing the eas - y way out,
she took me half the way there.
she on - ly played one-night stands.
Got a good rea - son
She's a big teas - er,
Tried to please her,

E7
for tak - ing the eas - y way out, now. She was a
she took me half the way there, now. She was a
she on - ly played one-night stands, now. She was a

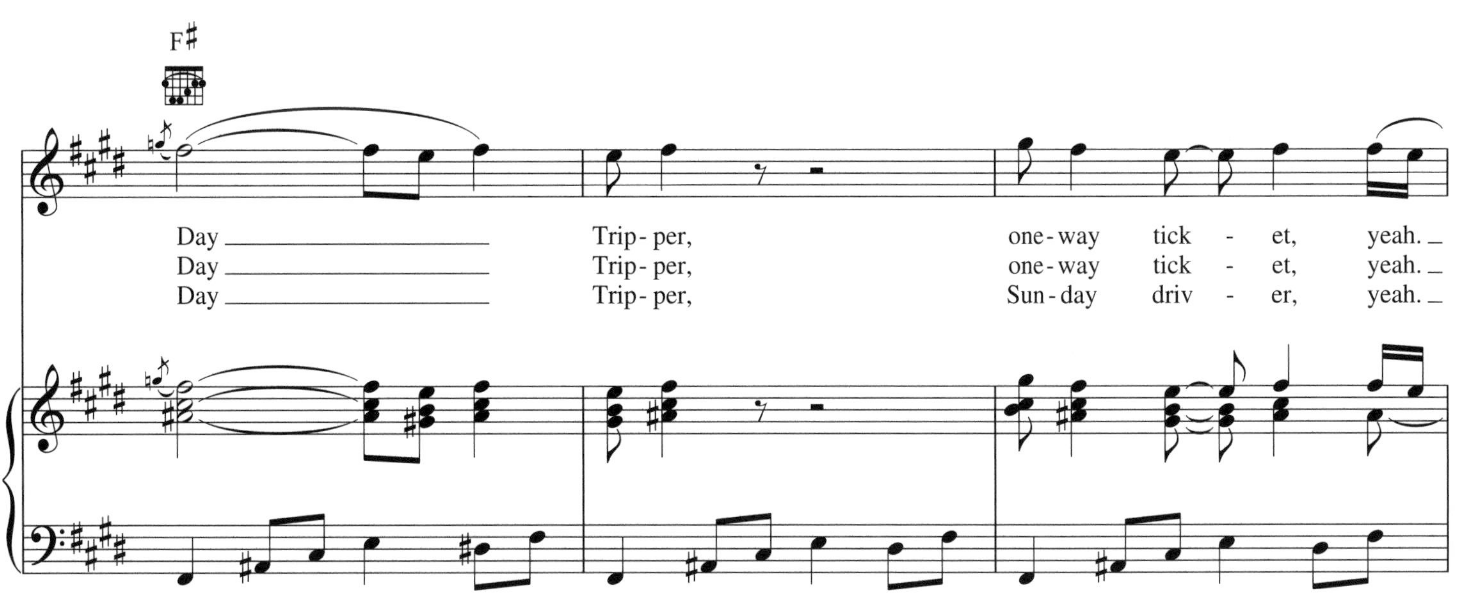
F♯
Day Trip - per, one-way tick - et, yeah.
Day Trip - per, one-way tick - et, yeah.
Day Trip - per, Sun - day driv - er, yeah.

A7
G♯7
4fr
It took me so long to find out,
It took me so long to find out,
It took me so long to find out,
C♯
To Coda
1
B
2
B
and I found out.
and I found out.
and I found
N.C.
B7
E/B
Ah
cresc.

F♯m/B
B6
A/B
B7
D.S. al Coda
CODA
B
N.C.
out.
Play 3 times
E7
Day Trip - per,
Repeat and Fade
Day Trip - per, yeah.

THE END

Words and Music by JOHN LENNON
and PAUL McCARTNEY

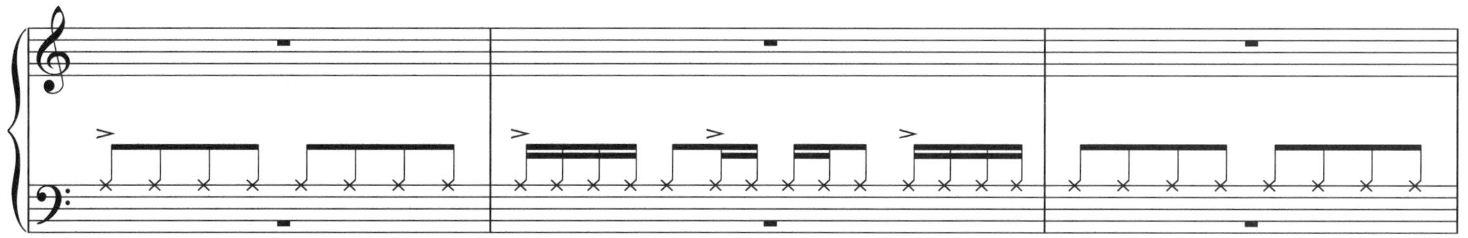

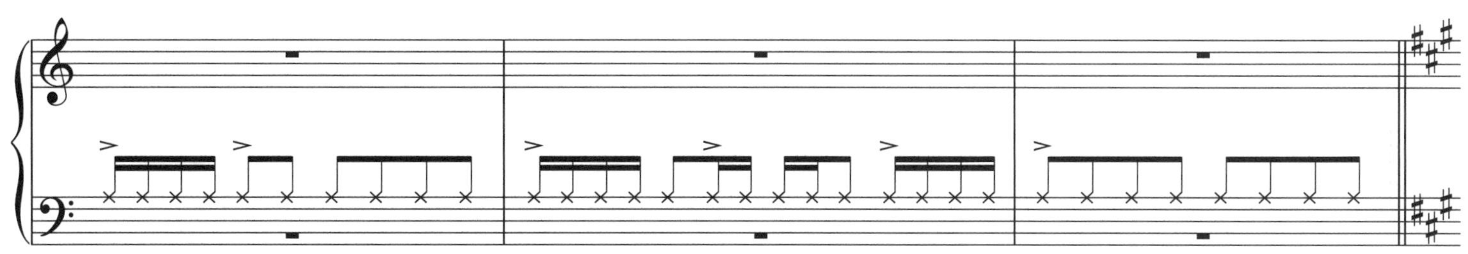

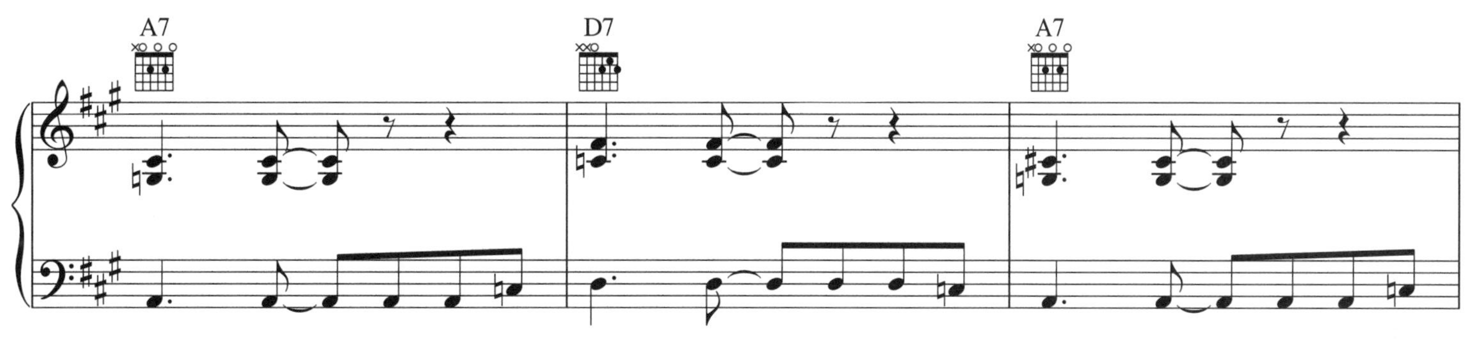
A7
D7
A7

D7
A7
D7
Love you, __
love you, __

A7
D7
A7
love you,
love you,
love you,
D7
A7
D7
love you,
love you,
love you,
A7
D7
A7
love you,
love you,
love you,
D7
A7
D7
love you,
love you,
love you,

A7
D7
A7
love you,
love you,
love you,
D7
A7
D7
love you,
love you,
love you,
A7
D7
A7
love you,
love you,
love you,
D7
A
love you.

G/A
D/A
G/A
3fr
3fr
And in the end, the love you take is equal to the love you make.
(♪ = ♪)
F
Em
Dm
Am/E
(♪ = ♪)
Dm
G7
C
D/C
Cm7
3fr
3
F/C
C

GET BACK

Words and Music by JOHN LENNON
and PAUL McCARTNEY

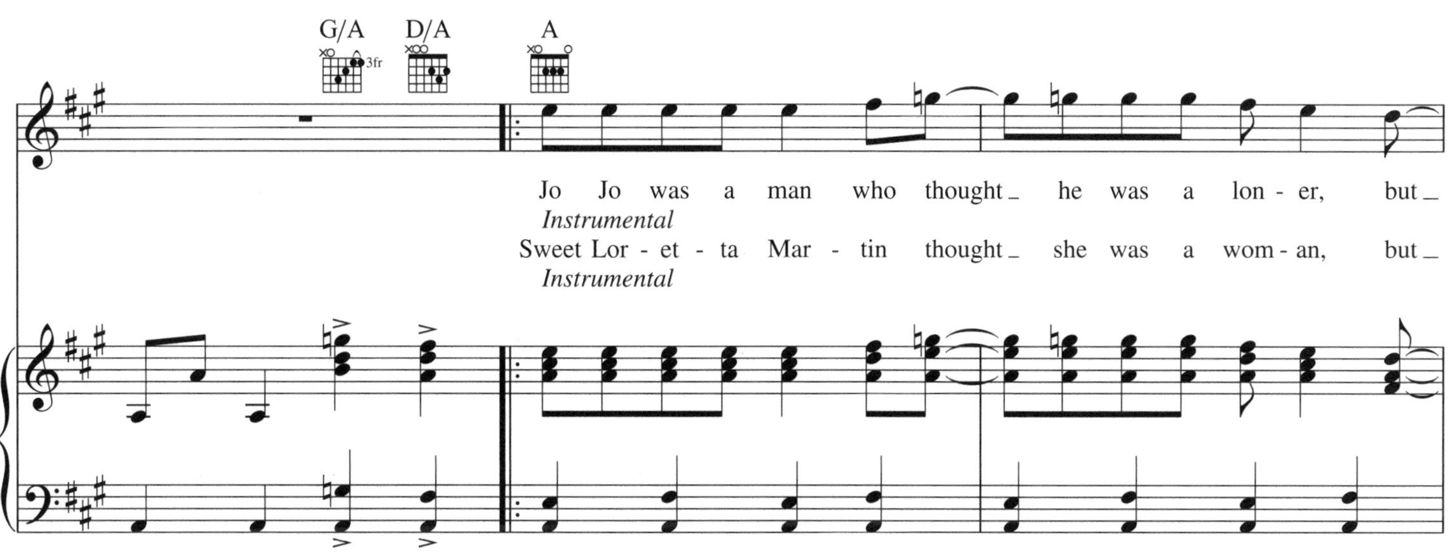

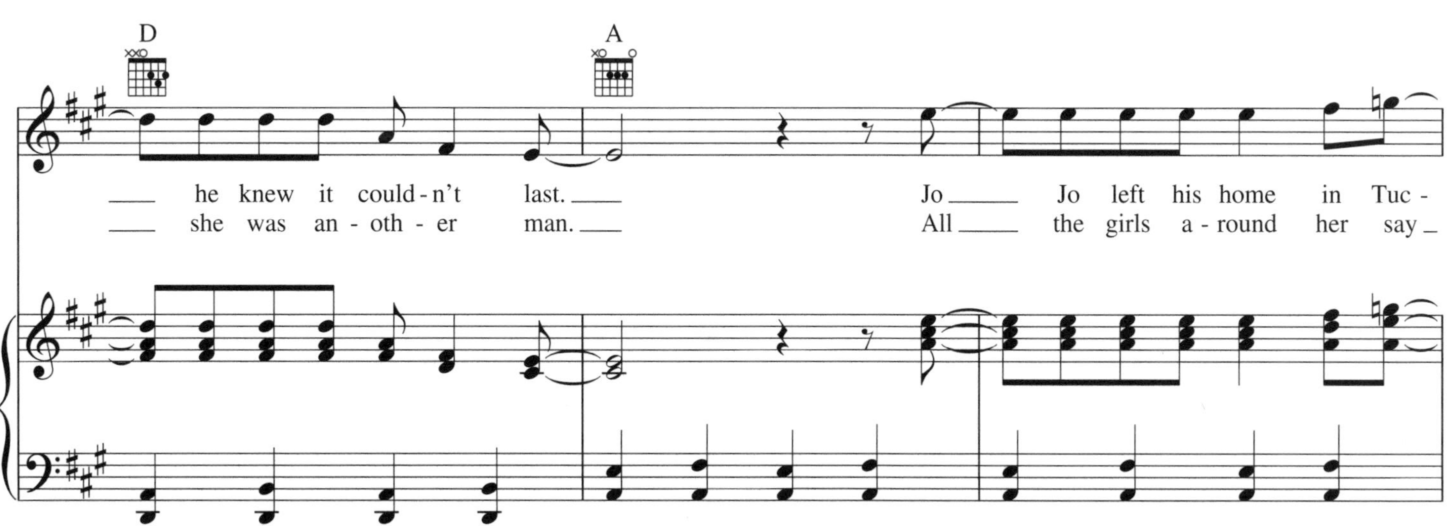

D
- son Ar - i - zo - na, for some Cal - i - for - nia grass.
she's got it com - ing, but she gets it while she can.
A
A7
End instrumental
End instrumental
Get back! Get back! Get back
D
A
G/A
3fr
D/A
A7
to where you once be - longed. Get back! Get back!
D
Get back to where you once be - longed.

1-3
A
(Get back, Jo Jo)
4
D7
A
Spoken ad lib:
Get back, Loretta, your momma's waitin' for you
Wearin' her high heel shoes and a low neck sweater.
Get back home, Loretta.
Repeat and Fade
D7
A
G/A
3fr
D/A

GIRL

Words and Music by JOHN LENNON
and PAUL McCARTNEY

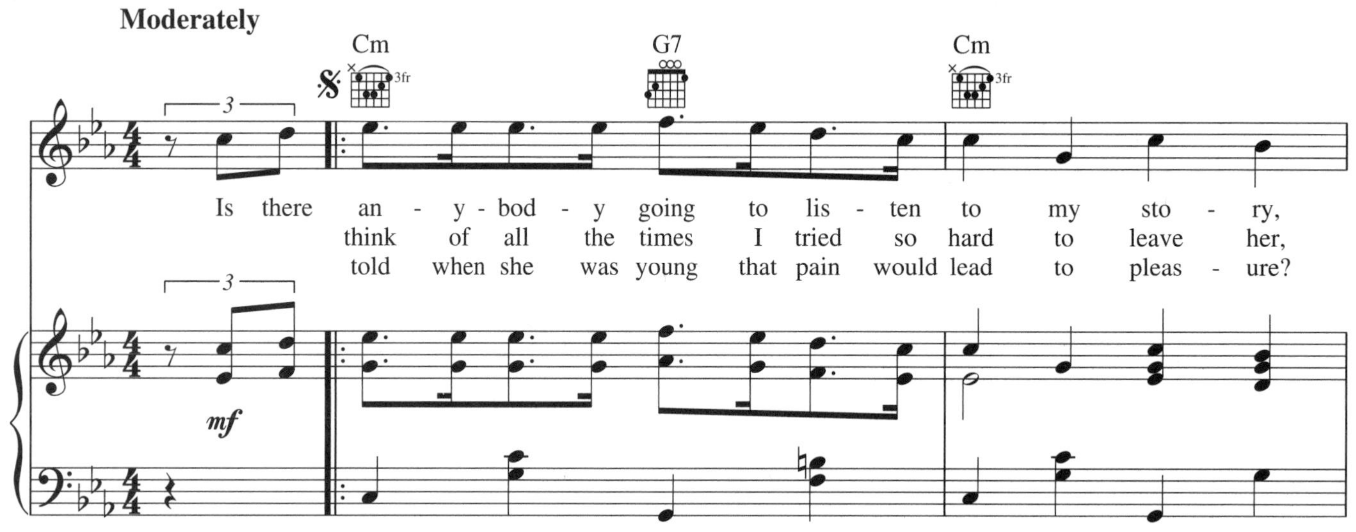

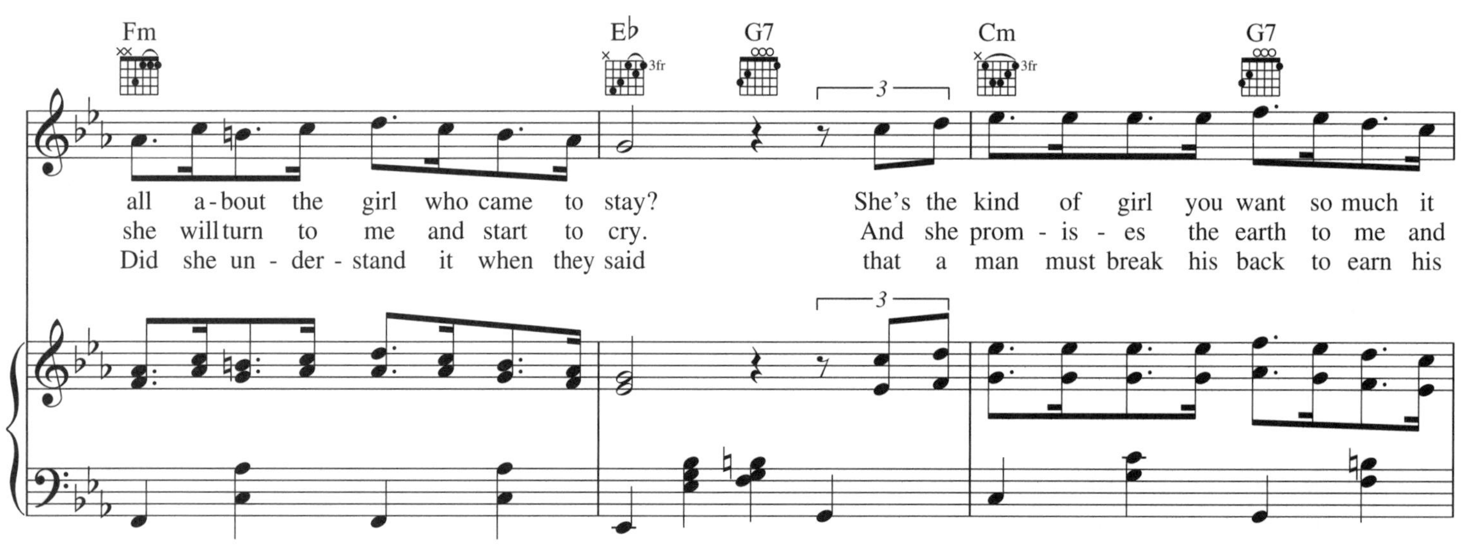

E♭
Gm/D
Fm/C
B♭7
E♭
Gm/D
3fr
3
girl,
girl,
girl.
3
1
2
Fm/C
B♭7
Fm/C
B♭7
Fm
3
When I
She's the kind of girl who puts you
3
L.H.
C
Fm
C
down when friends are there, you feel a fool.
Fm
C
When you say she's look - ing good, she acts as if it's un - der- stood. She's

Fm Ab Eb Gm/D

cool, ooh, ooh, ooh. Girl,

Fm/C Bb7 Eb Gm/D Fm/C Bb

D.S. al Coda

girl, girl. Was she

CODA

Eb Gm/D Fm/C Bb7 Eb Gm/D Fm/C Bb7

girl, girl.
Girl, girl.

Cm G7 Cm Fm Eb G7

Repeat and Fade

Instrumental

GIVE PEACE A CHANCE

Words and Music by
JOHN LENNON

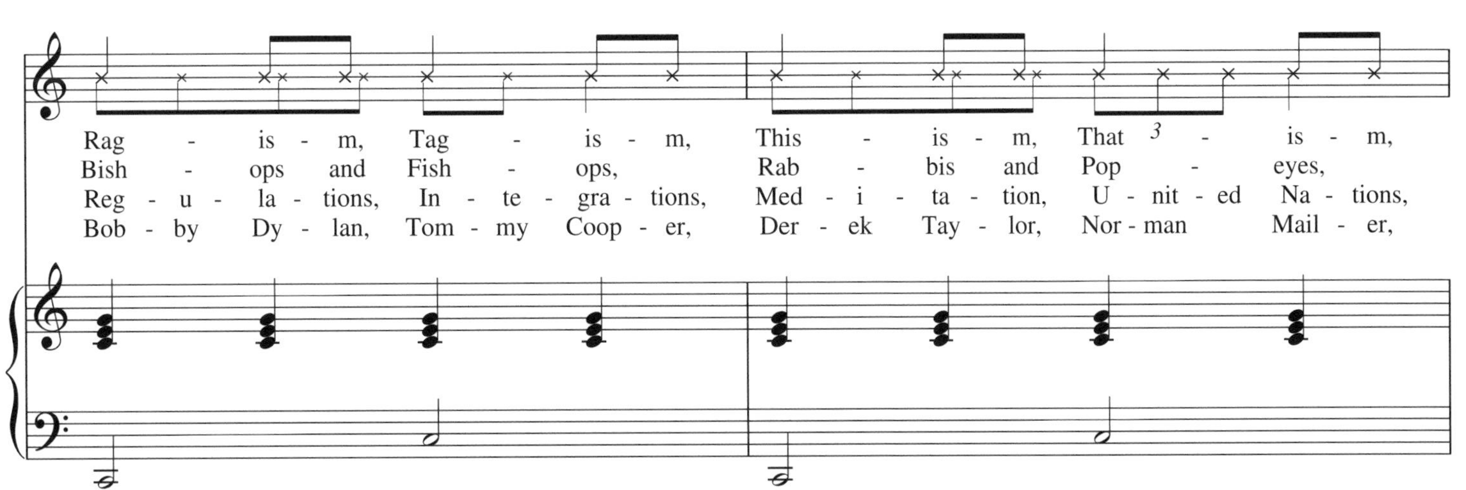

Is - n't it the most?
Bye - bye Bye - byes.
Con - grat - u - la - tions.
Al - len Gins - berg, Ha - re Krish - na Ha - re, Ha - re Krish - na,
All we are
G7
say - ing is give peace a
C
chance.
All we are
G7
say - ing is give peace a

C
1
chance.
C'- mon.
2
3
4
Let me tell you now.
Oh, let's stick to it.
All we are
G7
say - ing
is give peace a
C
Repeat ad lib. and Fade
chance.
All we are

A HARD DAY'S NIGHT

Words and Music by JOHN LENNON
and PAUL McCARTNEY

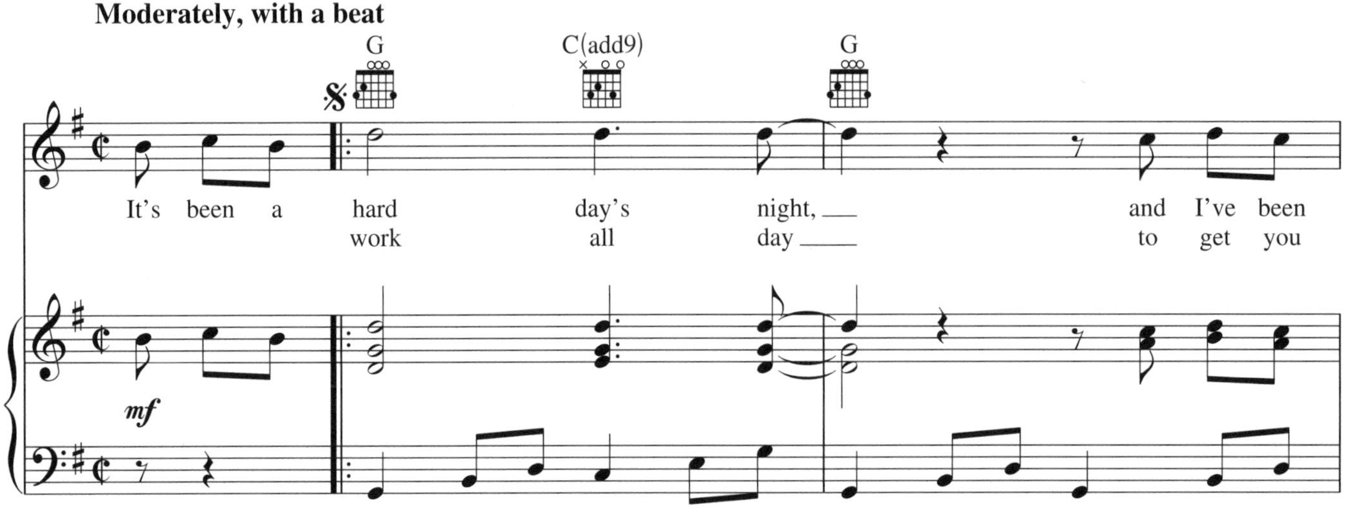

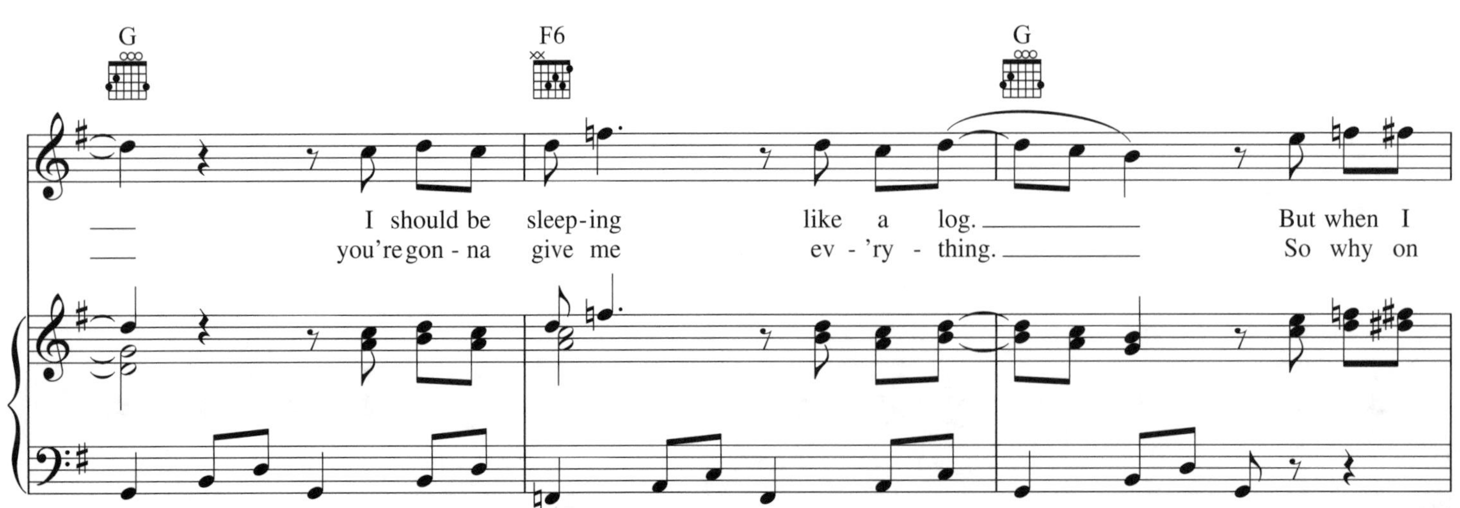

C
D
get home to you, I find the thing that you do will make me
earth should I moan, 'cause when I get you a - lone, you know I
G
C9
To Coda
1
G
2
G
feel al - right. You know, I
feel O - K. When I'm home,
Bm
Em
Bm
ev - 'ry - thing seems to be right.
G
Em
When I'm home, feel - ing you hold - ing me

C D G C(add9)
tight, tight, yeah. It's been a hard day's night,
G F6 G
and I've been work - ing like a dog.
It's been a
C(add9) G F6
hard day's night,
I should be sleep - ing like a log.
G C D
But when I get home to you,
I find the thing that you do
will make me

G
C9
G
D
G
C7
feel al - right.
G
F6
1
G
2
G
C
D
So why on earth should I moan, 'cause when I get you a - lone, you know I
G
C9
G
Bm
feel O - K. When I'm home,

Em
Bm
G
ev - 'ry-thing seems to be al - right.
When I'm home,
Em
C
D
D.S. al Coda
(Verse 1)
feel - ing you hold - ing me tight,
tight, yeah. It's been a
CODA
G
C9
G
You know I feel al - right.
You know I
C(add9)
F(add9)
Repeat and Fade
feel al - right.

HELLO, GOODBYE

Words and Music by JOHN LENNON
and PAUL McCARTNEY

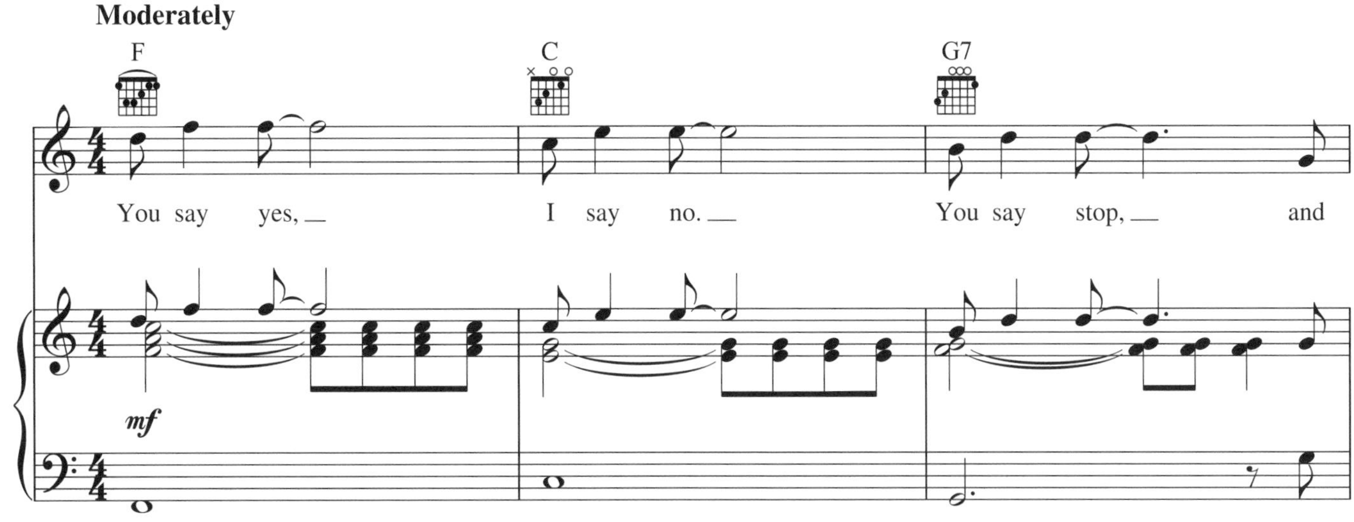

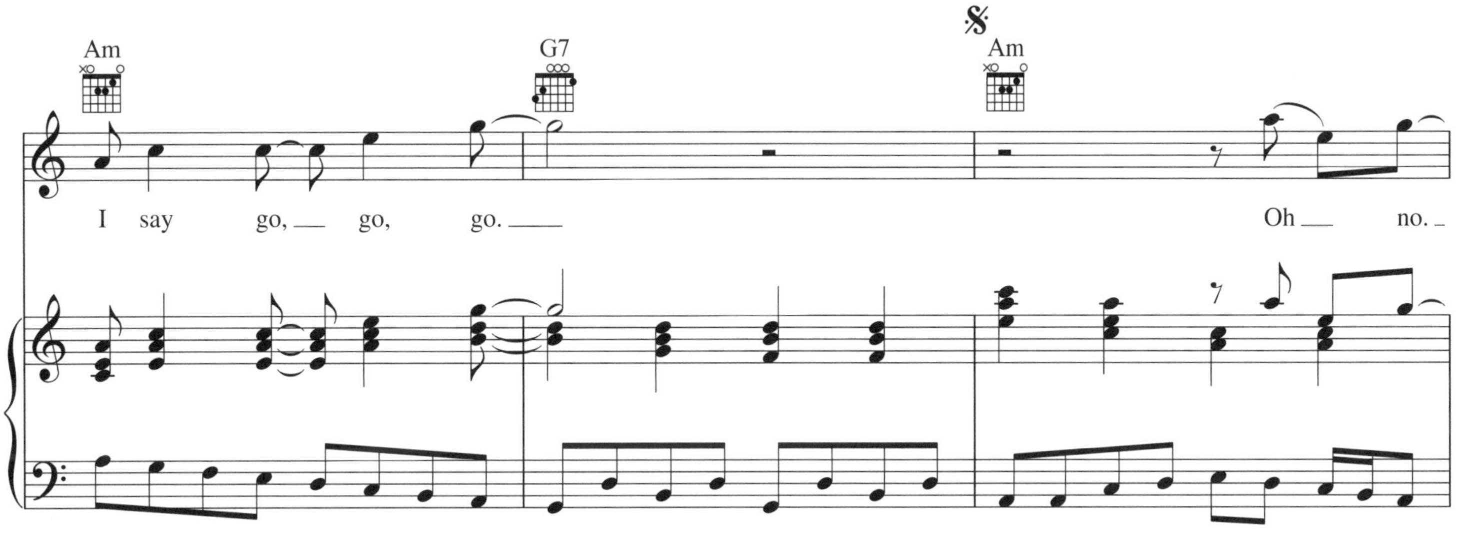

C
C/B
C/A
C/G
hel - lo, hel - lo. I don't know
F
A♭
4fr
C
C/B
why you say good - bye, I say hel - lo, hel - lo, hel - lo.
C/A
C/G
F
B♭
I don't know why you say good - bye, I say hel - lo.
C
F
C
I say high, you say low.
You say yes, I say no.

G7
Am
G7
You say why, and I say I don't know.
You say stop, and I say go, go, go.
Am
G
Oh, oh no.
G7
F/G
You say good - bye and I say hel - lo,
C
C/B
C/A
C/G
hel - lo, hel - lo. I don't know

F Ab C C/B

why you say good - bye, I say hel - lo, hel - lo, hel - lo.

C/A C/G F Bb

To Coda

I don't know why you say good - bye,
{ I say hel - lo.
{ I say hel - lo,

C F C

Why, why, why,

G7 Am G

D.S. al Coda

why, why, why, do you say good - bye, good - bye?

CODA
C
C/B
C/A
C/G
hel - lo, hel - lo. I don't know
F
A♭
4fr
A♭/G
why you say good - bye, I say hel - lo.
A♭/F♯
4fr
A♭/F
C
Hel - lo.
C
Repeat and Fade
Hey - la he - ba hel - lo - a.

HEY JUDE

Words and Music by JOHN LENNON
and PAUL McCARTNEY

C7
F
to make it bet - ter.
Hey
F
C
C7
C7sus
C7
Jude, don't be a - fraid.
Jude, don't let me down.
You were made to go out and
You have found her, now go and
F
B♭
get her.
get her.
The min - ute you let her un - der your
Re - mem - ber to let her in - to your
F
C7
F
skin, then you be - gin to make it bet - ter.
heart; then you can start to make it bet - ter.

F7 Bb Bb/A

And an - y - time you feel the pain, hey Jude, re - frain;
So let it out and let it in. Hey Jude, be - gin;

Gm7 Gm7/F C7/E C7 F

don't car - ry the world up - on your shoul - ders.
you're wait - ing for some - one to per - form with.

F7 Bb Bb/A

For well you know that it's a fool who plays it cool
And don't you know that it's just you? Hey Jude, you'll do.

Gm7 Gm7/F C7/E C7

by mak - ing his world a lit - tle cold -
The move - ment you need is on your shoul -

F
F7
C7
- er.
- der.
Da da da da da da da da da.
1
2
D.S. al Coda
Hey
Hey Jude,
CODA
C7
to make it bet-
F
- ter, bet - ter, bet - ter, bet - ter, bet - ter, bet - ter, oh.
Da da da
E♭
3fr
B♭
F
Optional Ending
Repeat and Fade
da da da da,
da da da da,
hey Jude.

I AM THE WALRUS

Words and Music by JOHN LENNON
and PAUL McCARTNEY

C
D
See how they run, like pigs from a gun, see how they fly. I'm
See how they smile, like pigs in a sty, see how they snied. I'm
A
A
A/G
cry - ing.
cry - ing.
Sit - ting on a corn - flake,
Yel - low mat - ter cus - tard,
Sem - o - li - na pil - chards
D/F♯
Fmaj7
G
A
A/G
wait - ing for the van to come.
drip - ping from a dead dog's eye.
climb - ing up the Eif - fel Tow - er.
F
Cor - por - a - tion tee shirt, stu - pid blood - y Tues - day man,
Crab - a - lock - er fish - wife por - no - graph - ic priest - ess, boy,
El - e - men - t'ry pen - guin sing - ing Ha - re Krish - na, Man,

B

you been a naught - y boy, you let your face grow long.
you been a naught - y girl, you let your knick - ers down.
you should have seen them kick - ing Ed - gar Al - lan Poe.

C

I am the egg - man, (Ooh) they are the

D

To Coda ⊕

E

egg - men, (Ooh) I am the wal - rus, Goo goo g' joob.

1

A A/G C D E

Mis - ter cit - y p'lice - man sit - ting pret - ty lit - tle p'lice - men in a row

A
A/G
C
See how they fly, like Lu - cy in the sky see how
D
A
they run
I'm cry - ing.
I'm
Dsus
A
cry - ing, I'm cry - ing,
I'm
E
D
D7
2
E
B
A
cry - ing.

G F E B A
Sit - ting in an Eng - lish gar -
G F E F
- den wait - ing for the sun.
If the sun don't come,
B7
you get a tan from stand - ing in the Eng - lish rain.
I am the
C D D7
egg - man.
They are the egg - men.
I am the

E
D
D.S. al Coda
wal - rus. Goo goo g' joob g' goo goo g' joob.
CODA
E
D
wal - rus, Goo goo g' joob, g' goo goo g' joob,
C
Bsus
Goo goo g' goo g' goo goo g' joob joob.
A
G
F
E7
Repeat and Fade

I FEEL FINE

Words and Music by JOHN LENNON
and PAUL McCARTNEY

D
said so. I'm in love with
said so. I'm in love with
said so. I'm in love with
C
B♭/C
1
G7
her and I feel fine.
her and I feel fine.
her and I feel fine.
2, 3
G7
G
I'm so
Bm
C
D
glad that she's my lit - tle girl,

G Bm C

she's so glad she's tell - ing all the world

D G7

that her ba - by buys her things you know, he

buys her dia - mond rings, you know she

D

said so. She's in love with

C
To Coda
G
D.S. al Coda
me and I feel fine.
CODA
G
D
C
G
She's in love with me and I feel fine.
Repeat and Fade

I SAW HER STANDING THERE

Words and Music by JOHN LENNON
and PAUL McCARTNEY

E
E7/G♯
A
how could I dance with an - oth - er, woo,
She would-n't dance with an - oth - er, woo,
C
E7
B7
when I saw her stand - ing there.
E7
1
2
Well, she
Well, my
A7
heart went boom when I crossed that room,

and I held her hand in
B7
A7
mine.
E7
Well, we danced through the night
Oh, we danced through the night
and we
A7
E7
held each oth - er tight,
and be - fore too long I

B7
fell in love with her.
Now
E
E7/G♯
A
I'll nev - er dance with an - oth - er, oh,
C
E7
B7
To Coda
since I saw her stand - ing there.
E7

B7

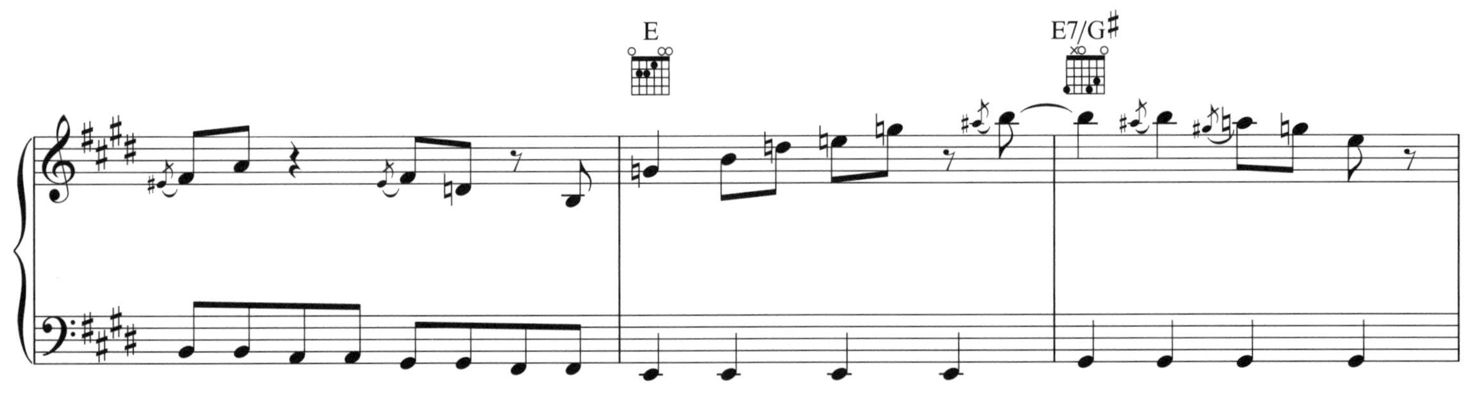
E
E7/G♯

A
E

B7
E7
D.S. al Coda
Well, my
CODA
E7
Oh, since I saw her
B7
E7
stand - ing there.
Yeah, well, since I saw her
B7
A
E
E9
stand - ing there.

I WANT TO HOLD YOUR HAND

Words and Music by JOHN LENNON
and PAUL McCARTNEY

Em
Bm
C
D
I want to hold your hand,
you'll let me hold your hand.
I want to hold your
Now let me hold your
G
Em
C
D
1 G
hand,
hand,
I want to hold your hand.
I want to hold your
Oh,
2
G
Dm7
G
hand.
And when I touch you I feel
more smoothly
C
Am
Dm7
hap - py in - side.
It's such a

G
C
D
C
D
feel - ing that my love I can't hide,
I can't hide,
C
D
I can't hide!
G
D
Yeah, you got that some - thing
Yeah, you got that some - thing
as before
Em
Bm
G
I think you'll un - der - stand. When I say that
I think you'll un - der - stand. When I feel that

D
Em
Bm
some - thing,
some - thing,
I want to hold your hand,
C
D
G
Em
1 C
D
I want to hold your hand,
I want to hold your
G
2
C
D
B7
hand.
I want to hold your hand,
C
D
C
G
I want to hold your hand.
3
3
3
3

I'M HAPPY JUST TO DANCE WITH YOU

Words and Music by JOHN LENNON
and PAUL McCARTNEY

E
G♯m7
F♯m7
B7
fun - ny, try and un - der - stand.
wan - na dance with you all night.
There is
In this
A
E
C♯m7
real - ly noth - ing else I'd rath - er do,
world there's noth - ing I would rath - er do,
'Cause I'm
A6
B+
E
B
E
hap - py just to dance with you.
I don't
you.
Just to
C♯m
F♯m
G♯
C♯m
dance with you
is ev - 'ry - thing I

F♯m G♯ C♯m
need. Be - fore this dance is through I think I'll
F♯m G♯7 A B7 E
love you too, I'm so hap - py when you dance with me. If some -
G♯m7 F♯m7 B7
bod - y tries to take my place, let's pre -
E G♯m7 F♯m7 B7
tend we just can't see his face. In this

A E C♯m7

world there's noth - ing I would rath - er do, 'Cause I'm / I've dis -

A6 B+ 1 E 2 C♯m

hap - py just to dance with you. Just to

cov - ered I'm in love with you.

F♯m G♯ A6 B+ C♯m

'Cause I'm hap - py just to dance with you.

F♯m7 G♯7 A6 B7 E6

Oh, oh, oh, oh, oh!

I'VE JUST SEEN A FACE

Words and Music by JOHN LENNON
and PAUL McCARTNEY

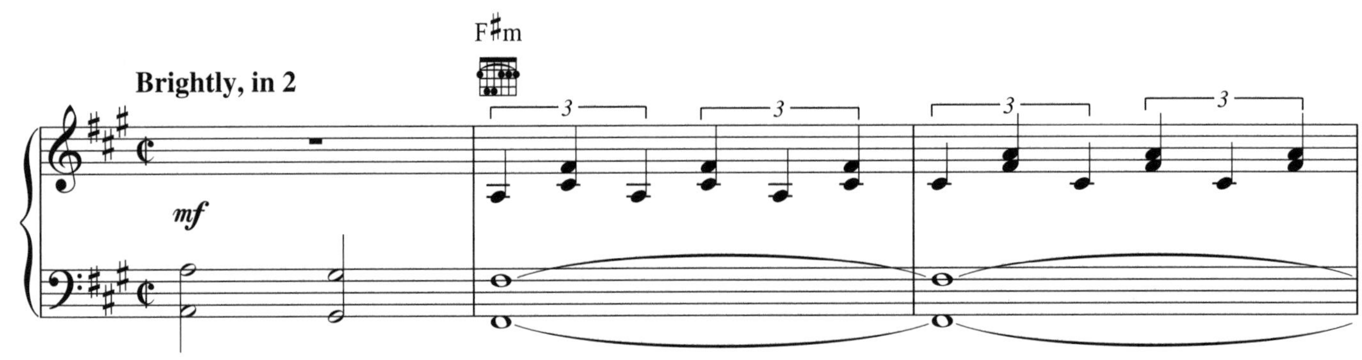

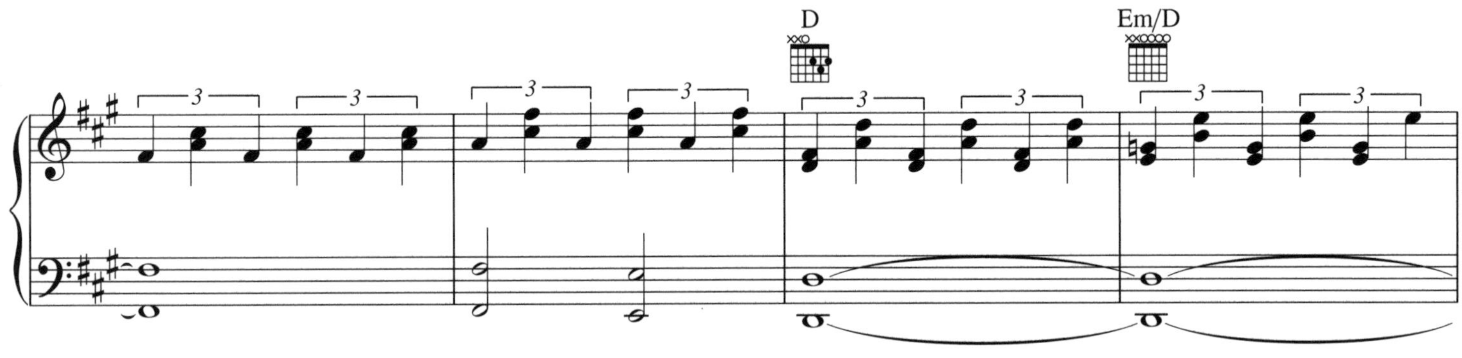

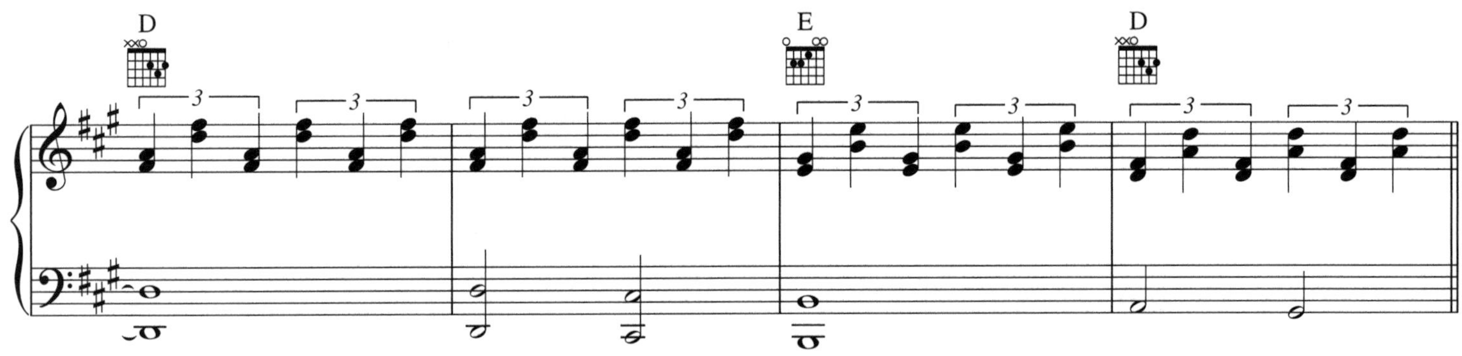

F♯m
place where we just met. She's just the girl for me and I
D
want all the world to see we've met. Mm mm
E
A
To Coda
mm mm mm.
Had it been an - oth - er day I
I have nev - er known the like of
Instrumental
F♯m
might have looked the oth - er way and I'd have nev - er been
this. I've been a - lone and I have missed things and kept out

a - ware. But, as it is, I'll dream of her to - night,
of sight, for oth - er girls were nev - er quite like this,
D
E
A
da da da da da da.
da da da da da da.
End instrumental
E
D
Fall - ing, yes, I am fall - ing, and she keeps
A
D
1, 2
A
call - ing me back a - gain.

3
A
D.S. al Coda
gain.
CODA
E
Fall - ing,
D
yes, I am fall - ing,
and she keeps
A
D
call - ing me back a - gain.
1, 2
A
3
N.C.
A
gain.

LET IT BE

Words and Music by JOHN LENNON
and PAUL McCARTNEY

Am
G
F
C
G
stand-ing right in front of me
speak-ing words of wis - dom; let it
F
C/E
Dm7
C
G/B
Am
G
be.
Instrumental ends
Let it be,
let it be,
let it be,
F
C
G
let it be.
Whis-per words of wis - dom; let it be.
F
C/E
Dm7
C
G
And when the bro - ken-heart - ed peo - ple
And when the night is cloud - y, there is

Am
G
F
C
G
liv - ing in the world a - gree there will be an an - swer, let it
still a light that shines on me. Shine un - til to - mor - row; let it
F
C/E
Dm7
C
G
be. For though they may be part - ed, there is
be. I wake up to the sound of mu - sic,
Am
G
F
C
G
still a chance that they will see there will be an an - swer; let it
Moth - er Mar - y comes to me speak ing words of wis - dom; let it
F
C/E
Dm7
C
G/B
Am
G
be.
be.
Let it be, let it be, let it be,

F
C
G
let it be.
There will be an an - swer; let it be.
F
C/E
Dm7
C
G/B
Am
G
Let it be, let it be, let it be,
F
C
G
To Coda
let it be.
Whis - per words of wis - dom; let it be.
There will be an an - swer; let it be.
F
C/E
Dm7
C
F
Em
Dm7
C
B♭
F/A

G F C F C G F C
D.S. al Coda
CODA
F C/E Dm7 C G/B Am G
Let it be, let it be, let it be,
F C G
let it be. Whis-per words of wis - dom; let it be.
F C/E Dm7 C F Em Dm7 C B♭ F/A G F C

MOTHER NATURE'S SON

Words and Music by JOHN LENNON
and PAUL McCARTNEY

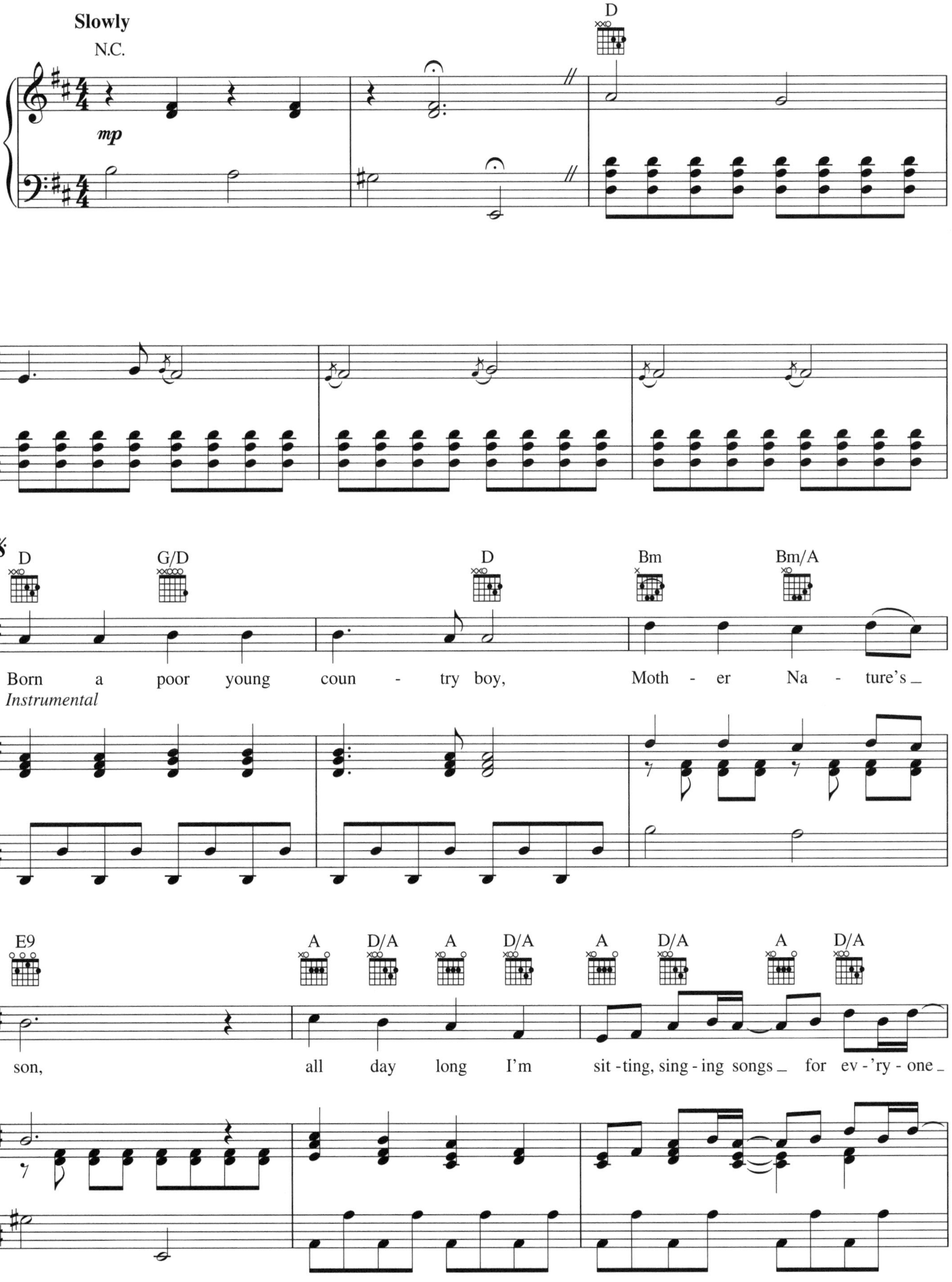

D G/D D Bm Bm/A

Born a poor young coun - try boy, Moth - er Na - ture's

Instrumental

E9 A D/A A D/A A D/A A D/A

son, all day long I'm sit - ting, sing - ing songs for ev - 'ry - one

D
Dm
G/D
D
To Coda
Dm
G/D
D
D
G/D
D
Sit be - side a moun - tain stream,
Find me in my field of grass,
Bm
Bm/A
E9
A
D/A
A
D/A
see her wa - ters rise;
Moth - er Na - ture's son.
Lis - ten to the
Sway - ing dais - es
A
D/A
A
D/A
D
Dm
pret - ty sound of mu - sic as she flies.
sing a la - zy song be - neath the sun.

G/D
D
G/D
D
Du du du du du du du du du du du
G/D
D
Dmaj7
du du du du du du du du du,
D7
Dsus
D7
G/D
Gm/D
1
D
du du du.
2
D
D.S. al Coda
CODA
D
Dm
G
D7
Hmm, Moth-er Na-ture's son.

NORWEGIAN WOOD
(This Bird Has Flown)

Words and Music by JOHN LENNON
and PAUL McCARTNEY

Em
F♯m7
B
I looked a-round and I no-ticed there was-n't a chair.
told her I did-n't and crawled off to sleep in the bath.
E
Bm7
A
E
I sat on a rug, bid-ing my time, drink-ing her wine.
And when I a-woke I was a-lone; this bird had flown.
Bm7
A
E
We talked un-til two and then she said, "It's time for bed."
So I lit a fire, is-n't it good Nor-we-gian wood.
Bm7
A
E
rit.

REVOLUTION

Words and Music by JOHN LENNON
and PAUL McCARTNEY

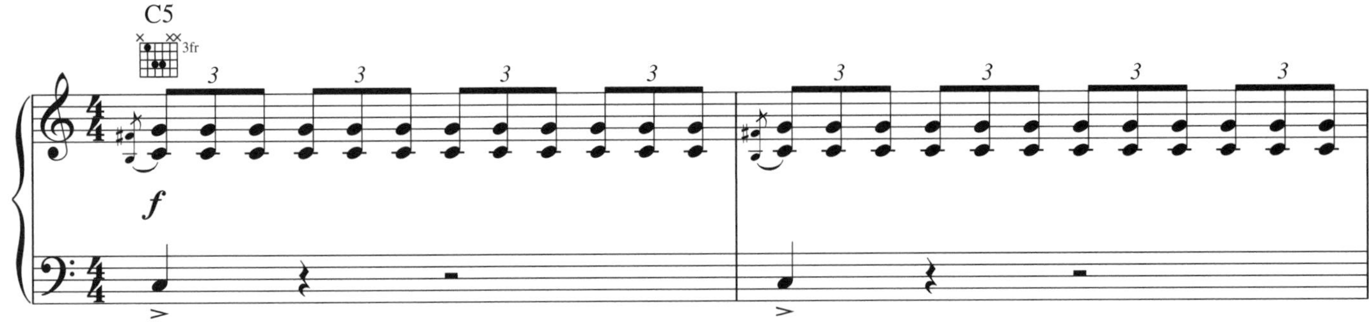

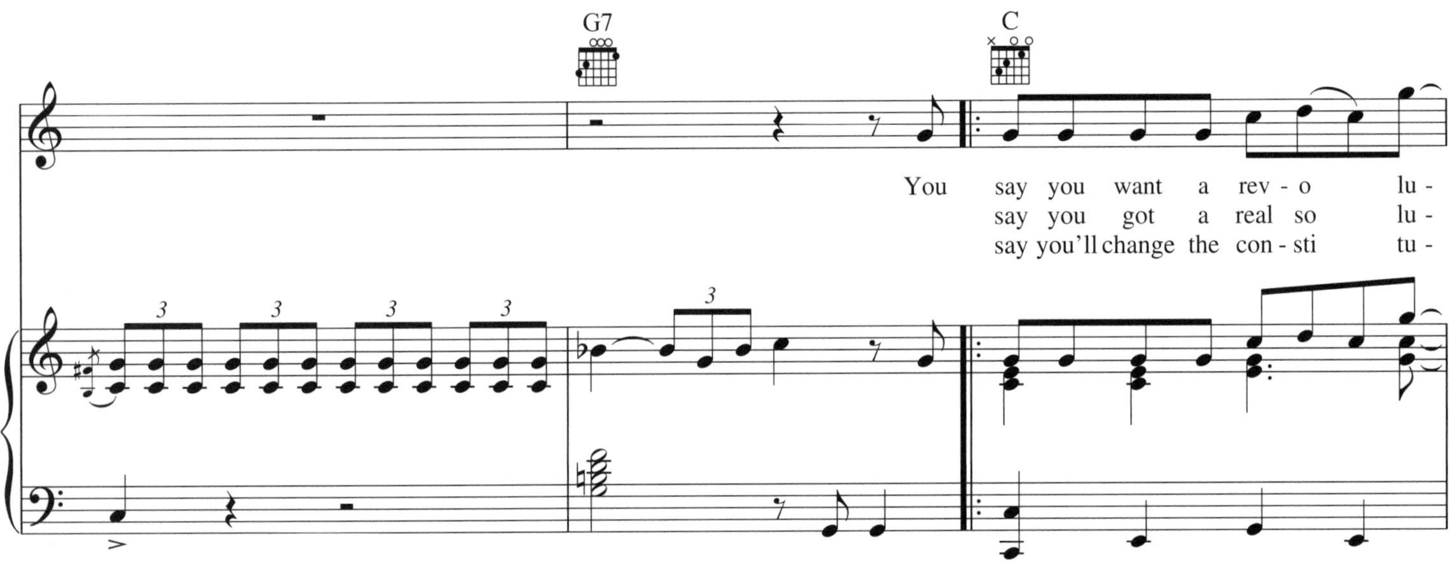

C
to change the world. You
to see the plan. You
to change your head. You
3
3
3
3
3

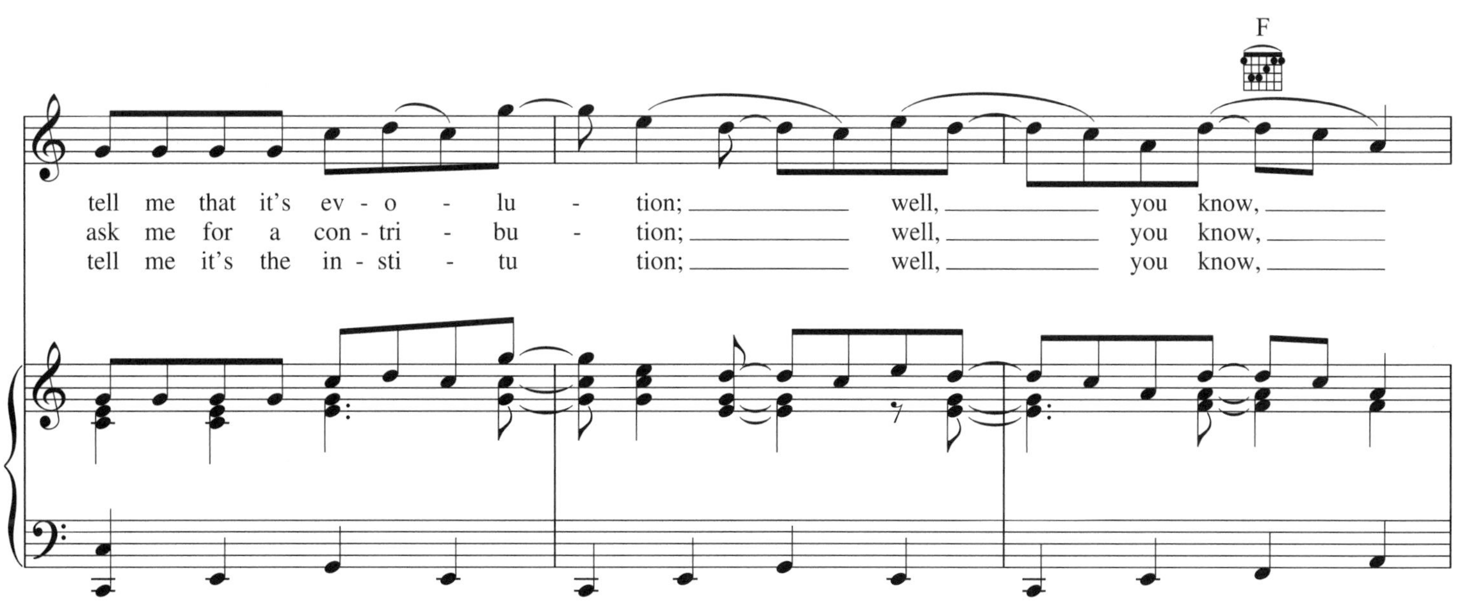
F
tell me that it's ev - o - lu - tion; well, you know,
ask me for a con - tri - bu - tion; well, you know,
tell me it's the in - sti - tu tion; well, you know,

G7
we all want to change the world.
we're all do - ing what we can.
you better free your mind in - stead.
3
3

Dm
G7
But when you talk a - bout de - struc - tion,
But if you want money for people with minds that hate,
But if you go carry - ing pictures of Chair-man Mao,
Dm
B♭
C
A
don't you know that you can count me out?
all I can tell you is, brother, you have to wait.
you ain't going to make it with any - one an - y - how.
G7sus
C
F6
Don't you know it's gon-na be al - right,
C
F(add2)
C
al - right,
al - right.

F(add2)
G7sus
1, 2
C/G
G7
You
You
3
C/G
G7
C
F
Al - right,
al - right,
al - right,
C
F
C
al - right,
al - right,
al - right,
F
G7
C
al - right,
al
right.

ROCKY RACCOON

Words and Music by JOHN LENNON
and PAUL McCARTNEY

Am7
D7sus
Rock - y Rac - coon checked in - to his room,
she and her man, who called him - self Dan,
L.H.
D7
G7
on - ly to find Gid - eon's Bi -
were in the next room at the hoe -
C
C/B
Am7
- ble. Rock - y had come, e -
- down. Rock - y burst in, and
D7sus
D7
G7
quipped with a gun, to shoot off the legs
grin - ning a grin, he said, "Dan - ny boy, this

C
C/B
of his ri - val.
is a show - down."
His
But
Am7
D7sus
D7
ri - val, it seems, had bro - ken his dreams, by
Dan - iel was hot, he drew first and shot, and
G7
C
C/B
steal - ing the girl of his fan - cy. Her
Rock - y col - lapsed in the cor - ner.
1
Am7
D7
name was Ma - gill, and she called her - self Lil, but

G7
C
C/B
ev - 'ry - one knew her as Nan - cy.
Now
2
Barrelhouse style
Am7
D7
G7
C
C/B
Am7
Now, the doc - tor came in,
L.H.

D7sus
D7
stink - ing of gin, and pro -
G7
C
C/B
ceed - ed to lie on the ta - ble. He said,
Am7
D7sus
"Rock - y, you met your match," and Rock - y said, "Doc, it's on - ly a scratch,
D7
G7
and I'll be bet - ter, I'll be bet - ter, Doc, as soon as I am

C
C/B
Am7
a - ble." Now Rock - y Rac - coon, he fell
D7
G7
back in his room, on - ly to find
C
C/B
Am7
Gid - eon's Bi - ble. Gid - eon checked out
D7sus
D7
and he left it no doubt to

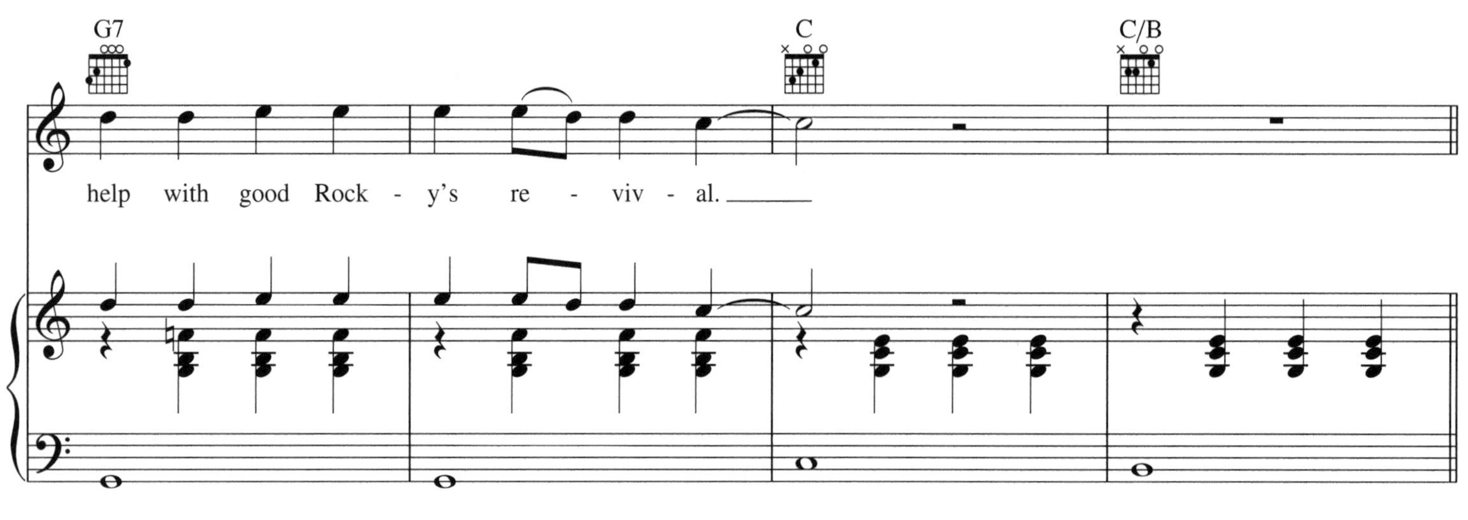
G7
C
C/B
help with good Rock - y's re - viv - al.

Barrelhouse style
Am7
D7

G7

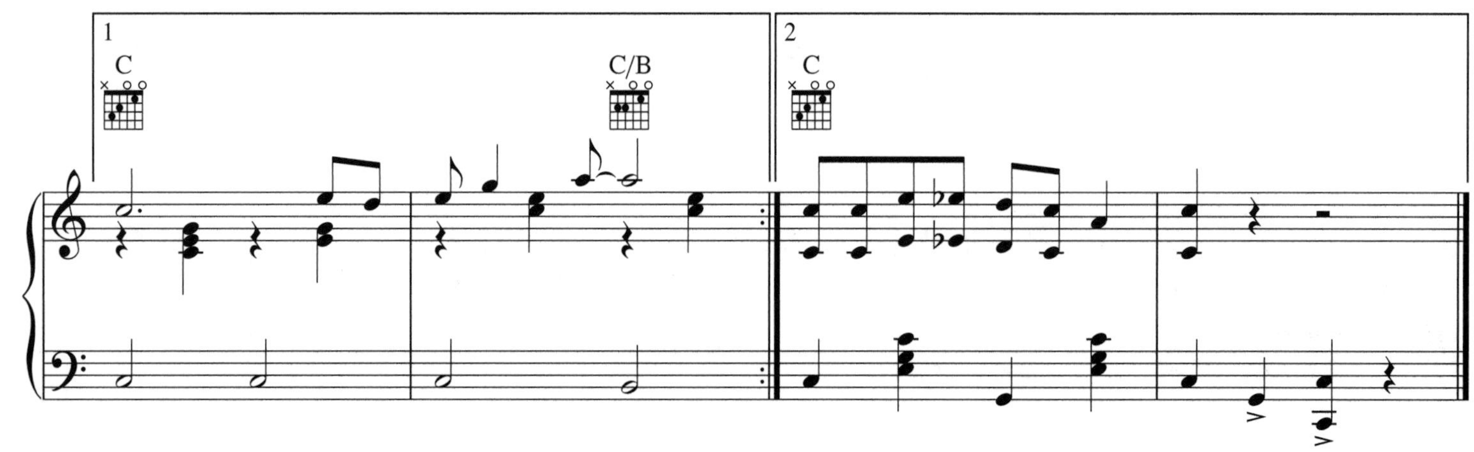
1
C
C/B
2
C

SGT. PEPPER'S LONELY HEARTS CLUB BAND

Words and Music by JOHN LENNON
and PAUL McCARTNEY

A7
C
may I in - tro - duce to you
the act you've known for all these years:
let me in - tro - duce to you
the one and on - ly Bil - ly Shears.
G
C
G
C7
Ser - geant Pep - per's Lone - ly Hearts Club Band.
F
C
D7
G
B♭
F
We're Ser - geant Pep - per's Lone - ly Hearts
We're Ser - geant Pep - per's Lone - ly Hearts

C
G
C
G
Club Band, we hope you will en - joy the show.
Club Band. We hope you have en - joyed the show.
B♭
F
C
G
Ser - geant Pep - per's Lone - ly Hearts Club Band, sit
Ser - geant Pep - per's Lone - ly Hearts Club Band, we're
A7
D7
C
G
back and let the eve - ning go. Ser-geant Pep-per's Lone - ly, Ser -
sor - ry but it's time to go. Ser-geant Pep-per's Lone - ly, Ser -
A7
C
- geant Pep - per's Lone - ly, Ser - geant Pep - per's Lone - ly Hearts
- geant Pep - per's Lone - ly, Ser - geant Pep - per's Lone - ly Hearts

C/D G
1
C F7
Club Band. It's won-der-ful to be here, it's cer-tain-ly a thrill, you're
Club Band.
C D7
such a love-ly au-di-ence, we'd like to take you home with us, we'd love to take you home. I don't
2
G B♭ F C G C
Ser-geant Pep-per's Lone-ly Hearts Club Band. We'd like to thank you once a-gain.
G B♭ F C G
Ser-geant Pep-per's one and on-ly Lone-ly Hearts Club Band. It's

A7 D7 C G

get - ting ver - y near the end. Ser-geant Pep-per's Lone - ly, Ser -

A7 C

- geant Pep - per's Lone - ly, Ser - geant Pep - per's Lone - ly Hearts

G

Club Band.

B♭ C G

STRAWBERRY FIELDS FOREVER

Words and Music by JOHN LENNON
and PAUL McCARTNEY

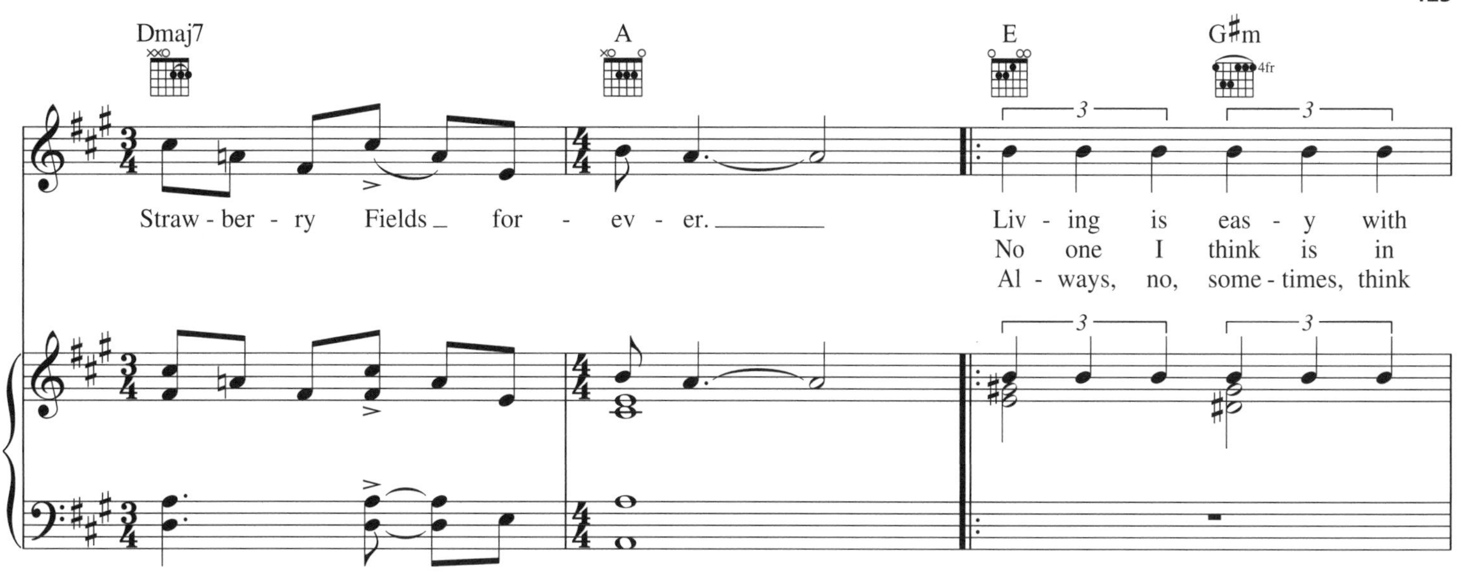
Dmaj7
A
E
G♯m
4fr
Straw - ber - ry Fields for - ev - er.
Liv - ing is eas - y with
No one I think is in
Al - ways, no, some - times, think

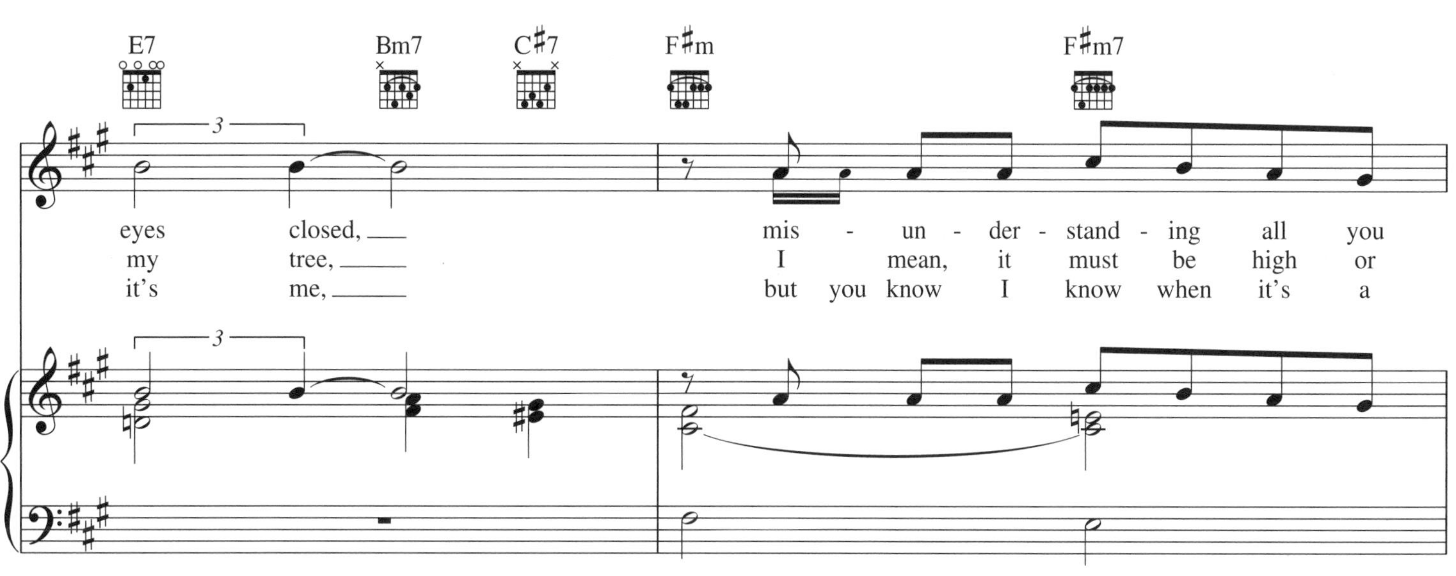
E7
Bm7
C♯7
F♯m
F♯m7
eyes closed,
my tree,
it's me,
mis - un - der - stand - ing all you
I mean, it must be high or
but you know I know when it's a

Dmaj7
D
E7
see.
low.
dream.
It's get - ting hard to be some -
That is, you can't, you know, tune
I think a "No," I mean a

A
F♯m
D
E
one, but it all works out; it does-n't mat-ter much to
in, but it's all right. That is, I think it's not too
"Yes," but it's all wrong. That is, I think I dis-a-

D
A
me.
bad.
gree.
Let me take you down, 'cause I'm go-ing to

Em7
C♯dim
4fr
Straw-ber-ry Fields. Noth-ing is real, and

D
E
F#
1, 2
Dmaj7
noth - ing to get hung a - bout.
Straw - ber - ry Fields for -
A
3
Dmaj7
ev - er.
Straw - ber - ry Fields for -
A
F#m
Dmaj7
A
ev - er,
Straw - ber - ry Fields for - ev - er,
Dmaj7
E
D
A
Straw - ber - ry Fields for - ev - er.

THIS BOY
(Ringo's Theme)

Words and Music by JOHN LENNON
and PAUL McCARTNEY

1
Dmaj7
Bm
Em
A7
gain.
2
Dmaj7
D
D7
gain.
Oh, and
G
F♯7
this boy would be hap - py, just to
Bm
D7
love you, but oh my! Oh,

G
E7
that boy won't be hap - py
A7
A7sus
A7
F♯m/A
A
till he's seen you cry.
Dmaj7
Bm
Em
A7
This boy would - n't mind the
Dmaj7
Bm
Em
A7
pain, would al - ways feel the

Dmaj7
Bm
Em7
A7
same
if this boy gets you back a-
Dmaj7
Bm
Em
A7
gain.
Dmaj7
Bm
Em
A7
This boy.
Dmaj7
Bm
Em
A7
Repeat and Fade
This boy.

TILL THERE WAS YOU

Words and Music by
MEREDITH WILLSON

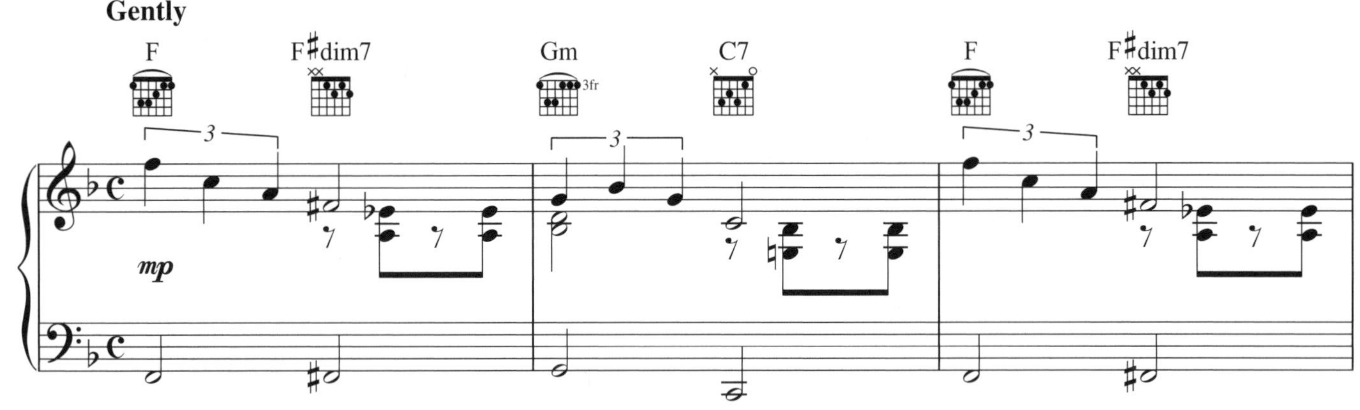

Gm7 Gm7/C C7
1
F Gm7 C7
all till there was you. There were
all till
2
F F7 B♭
there was you. Then there was mu - sic
B♭m F D7
and won - der - ful ros - es, they tell me, in
Gm7 G7 C7
sweet, fra - grant mea - dows of dawn and

C+
F
F♯dim7
dew. There was love all a - round but I
Gm7
B♭m
F
F/A
A♭m6
4fr
nev - er heard it sing - ing, No, I nev - er heard it at
Gm7
Gm7/C
C7
F
To Coda
Gm7
C7
all, till there was you.
F
F♯dim7
Gm7

B♭m
F
Am7
A♭m7
4fr
Gm7
G♭7♯9
3fr
F
Cdim7
F7
D.S. al Coda
Then there was
CODA
F
C7
C+
C7
F
Till
there was you.
D♭7
4fr
F
Fmaj7

TWIST AND SHOUT

Words and Music by BERT RUSSELL
and PHIL MEDLEY

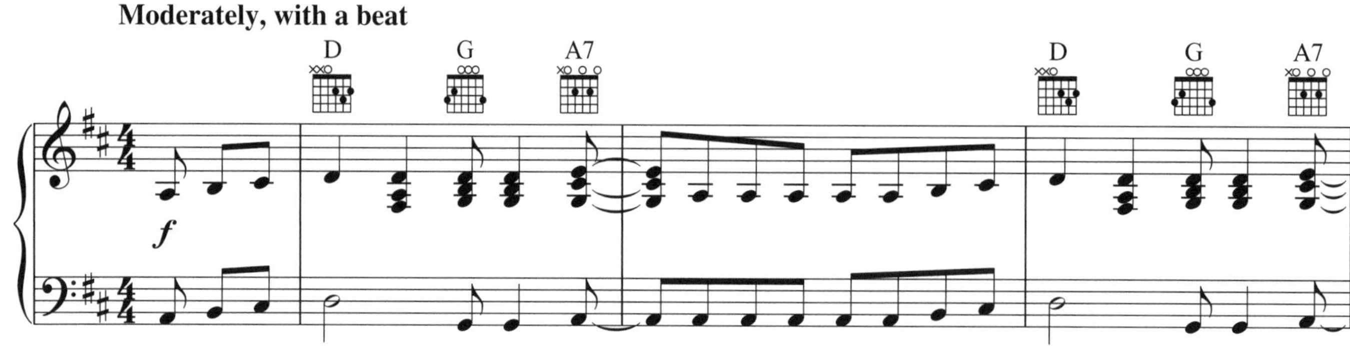

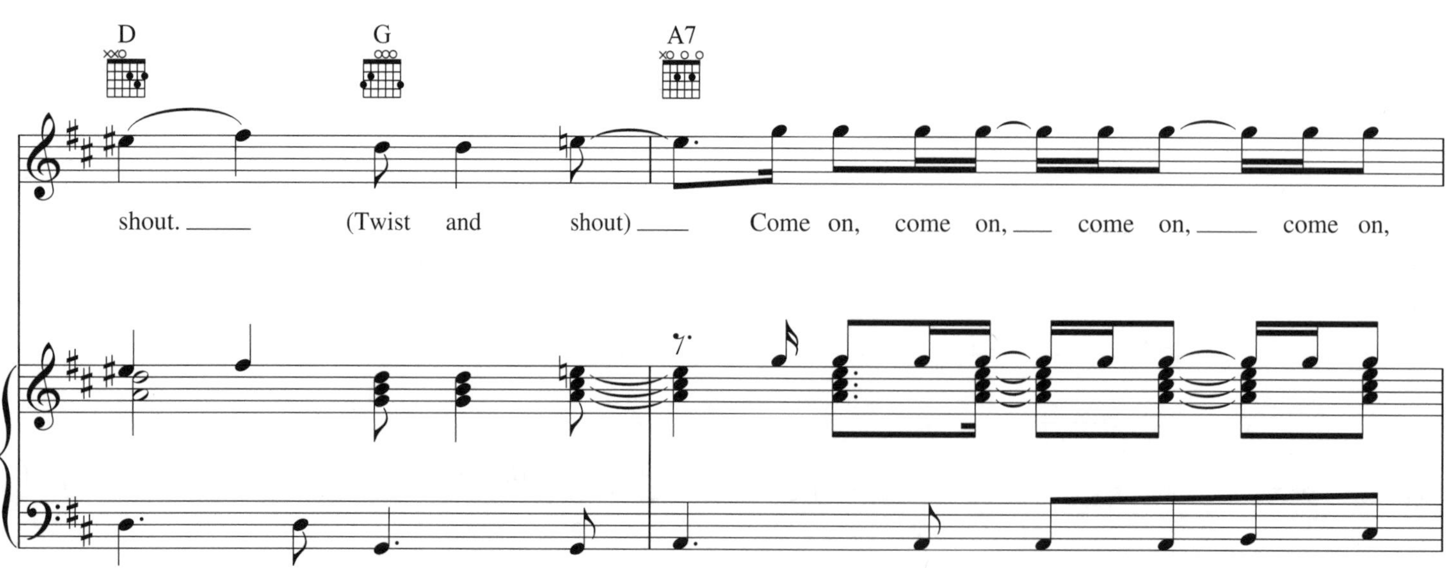

D
G
A7
ba - by, now, Come on and work it on out.
(Come on, ba - by)
(Work it on out)
(1.) Well, work it on out,
(2., 3.) You know you twist, lit - tle girl,
(Work it on out)
(Twist, lit - tle girl)
You know you look so good.
You know you twist so fine.
(Look so good)
(Twist so fine)
You know you got me
Come on and twist a lit - tle
go - in' now, (Got me goin')
clos - er now, (Twist a lit - tle clos - er)
Just like I knew you would.
And let me know that you're

D
G
To Coda
1
A7
2
A7
(Like I knew you would)
Well, shake it up ba -
mine. (Let me know you're mine)
D
G
A
G
A
D
G
A
G
A
D
G
A
G
A
D
G
A
G
A
Ah
Ah

A7
D.S. al Coda
Ah
Ah
Ah
Shake it up ba-
CODA
A7
D
G
Well, shake it, shake it, shake it, ba - by, now,
(Shake it up ba -
A7
D
G
A
Well, shake it, shake it, shake it, ba-by, now.
- by)
(Shake it up, ba - by.)
Ah
A7
D
Dmaj9
4fr
Ah
Ah
Ah

TWO OF US

Words and Music by JOHN LENNON
and PAUL McCARTNEY

Bm
Am
earned pay.
my wall.
the sun.
G
You and me, Sun - day driv - ing,
You and me, burn - ing match - es,
You and me, chas - ing pa - per,
C
not ar - riv - ing on
lift - ing latch - es on
get - ting no - where on
Bm
Am
our way back
our way back
our way back

G
D7
home.
home.
home.
We're on our way
G
D7
home,
We're on our way
G
D7
home.
We're go - in'
G
To Coda
1
2, 3
home.

B♭
You and I
Dm
have mem - o - ries
Gm
3fr
long - er than the road
Am
that stretch -
- es out a - head.
D11
5fr

D7
1
D.S.
2
D.S. al Coda
CODA
N.C.
(Spoken:) We're goin' home.
G
Repeat and Fade
Better believe it.
Goodbye.

WE CAN WORK IT OUT

Words and Music by JOHN LENNON
and PAUL McCARTNEY

Bm
Bm/A
Bm/G
Life is ver - y short, and there's no time
F♯sus
F♯
Bm
Bm/A
for fuss - ing and fight - ing, my friend.
Bm/G
Bm/F♯
Bm
Bm/A
I have al - ways thought that it's a crime,
Bm/G
F♯sus
F♯
Bm
Bm/A
so I will ask you once a -

Bm/G
Bm/F#
D
Dsus
D
gain.
Try to see it my way,
Dsus
C(add9)
D
Dsus
D
on-ly time will tell if I am right or I am wrong.
While you see it your way,
Dsus
C(add9)
D
G
D
there's a chance that we might fall a-part be-fore too long.
We can work it out,
G
Asus
A
D
G6/D
3fr
D
we can work it out.

WITH A LITTLE HELP FROM MY FRIENDS

Words and Music by JOHN LENNON
and PAUL McCARTNEY

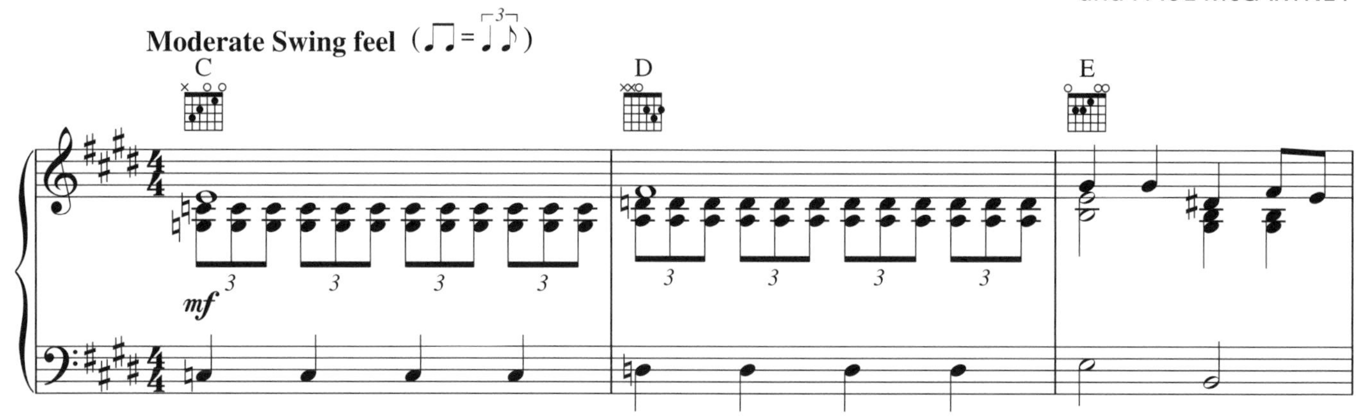

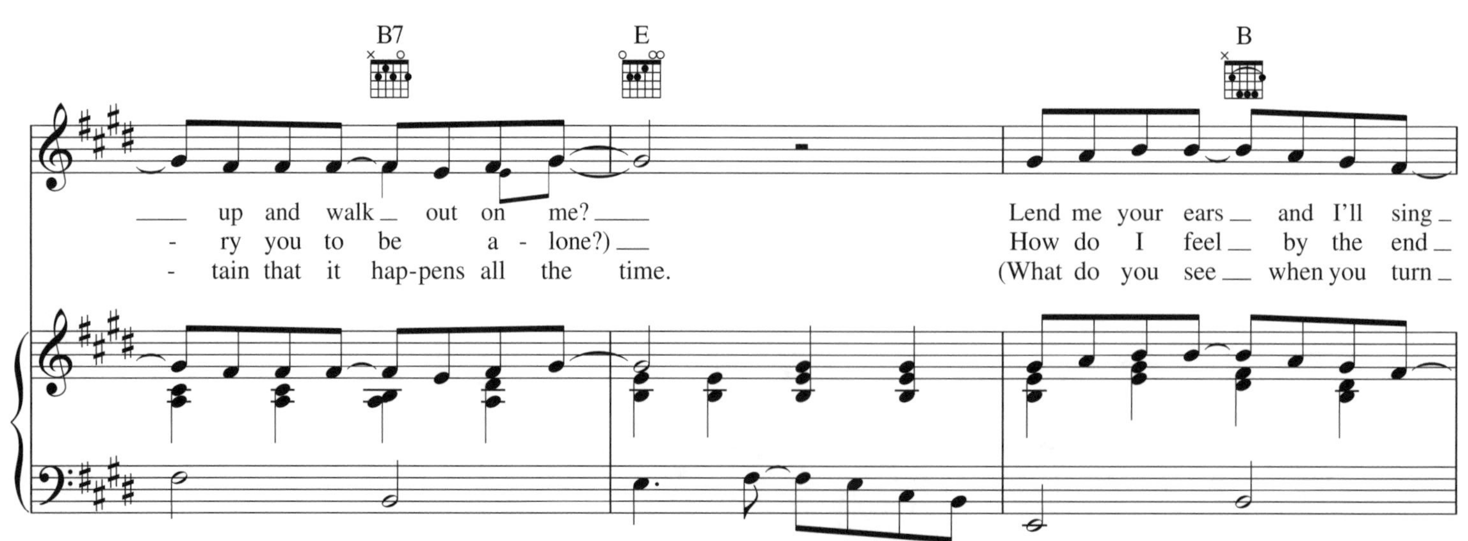

F♯m
B7
you a song, and I'll try not to sing out of key.
of the day? (Are you sad be - cause you're on your own?)
out the light?) I can't tell you, but I know it's mine.

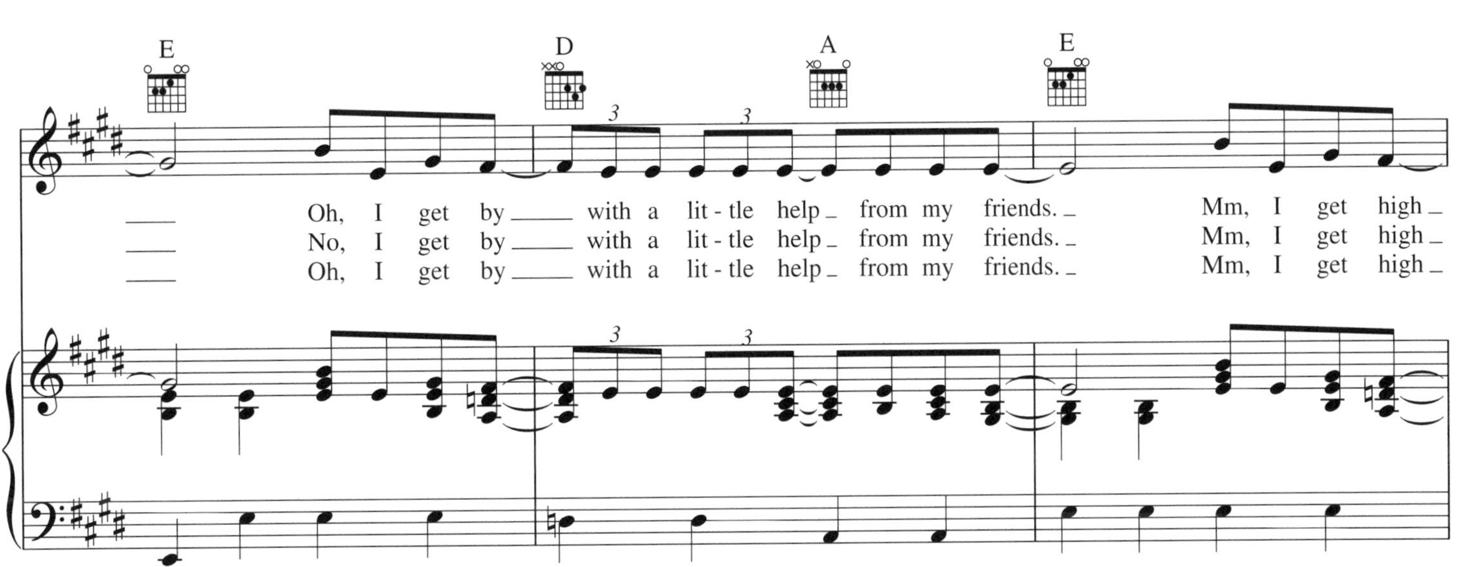
E
D
A
E
Oh, I get by with a lit - tle help from my friends. Mm, I get high
No, I get by with a lit - tle help from my friends. Mm, I get high
Oh, I get by with a lit - tle help from my friends. Mm, I get high

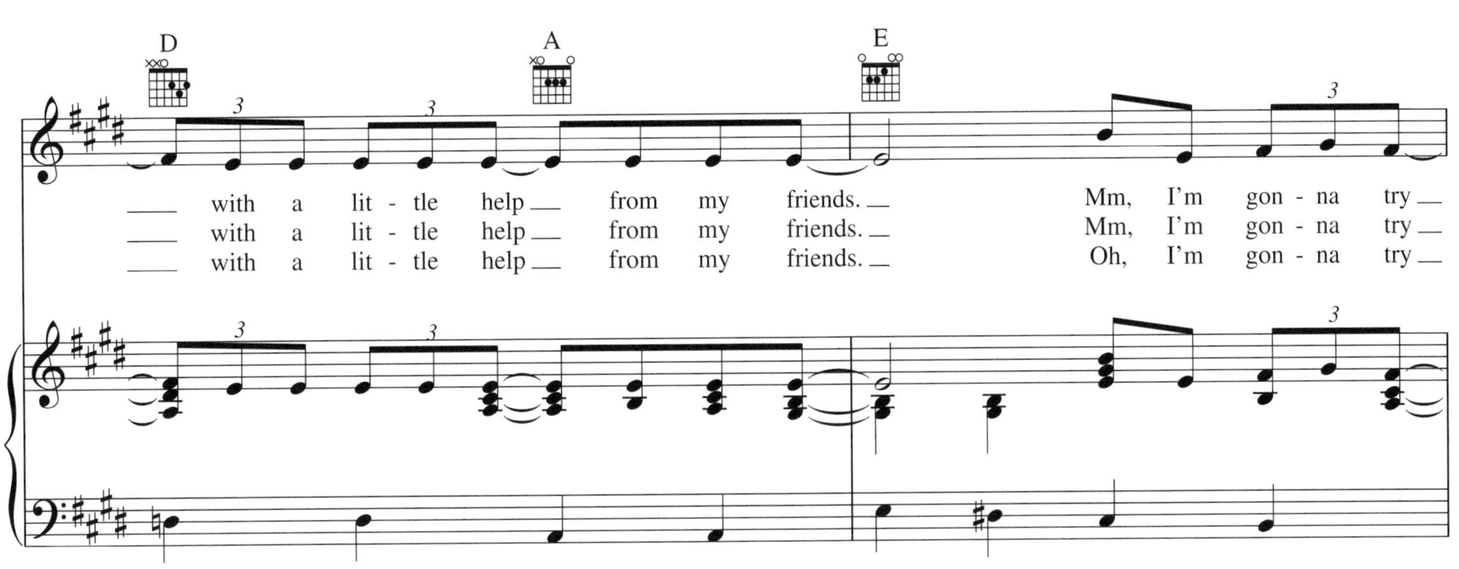
D
A
E
with a lit - tle help from my friends. Mm, I'm gon - na try
with a lit - tle help from my friends. Mm, I'm gon - na try
with a lit - tle help from my friends. Oh, I'm gon - na try

1
A
E
B7
with a lit - tle help from my friends.
with a lit - tle help from my friends.
with a lit - tle help from my friends.
2, 3
E
C♯m
F♯7
(Do you need any - y - bod - y?) I
(Do you need any - y - bod - y?) I
E
D
A
C♯m
need some - bod - y to love. (Could it be an - y - bod -
just need some - one to love. (Could it be an - y - bod -
F♯7
To Coda
E
D
A
D.S. al Coda
(take 2nd ending)
- y?) I want some - bod - y to love.
- y?) I want some - bod - y to love.

CODA
A
D
A
Oh, I get by with a lit-tle help from my friends.
E
D
A
E
Mm, I'm gon-na try with a lit-tle help from my friends.
Oh, I get high
A
E
D
with a lit-tle help from my friends.
Yes, I get by with a lit-tle help from my friends,
A
C/G
Am6
E
with a lit-tle help from my friends.

YESTERDAY

Words and Music by JOHN LENNON
and PAUL McCARTNEY

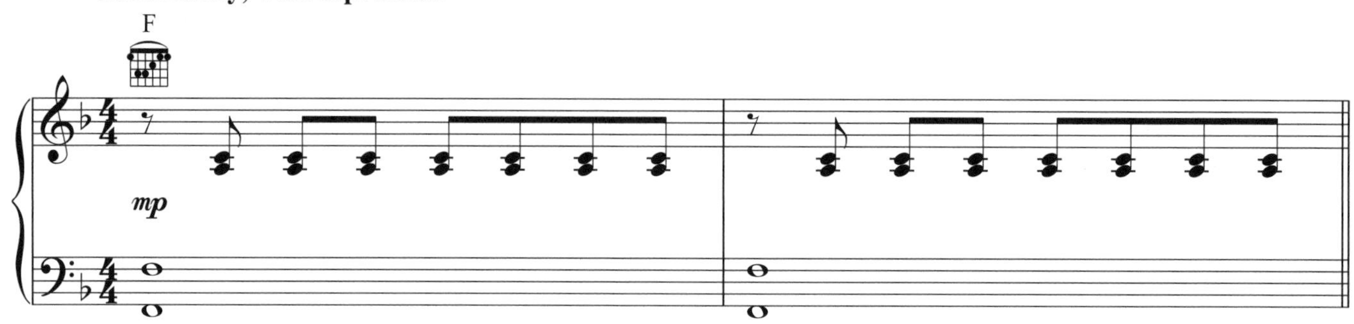

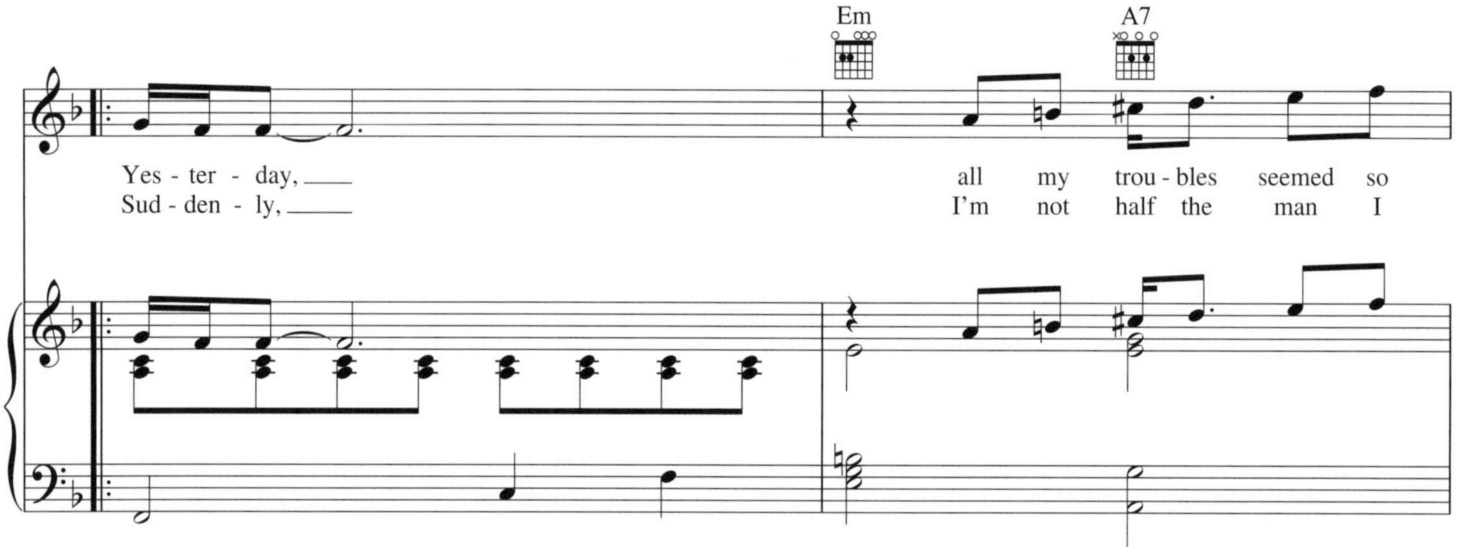

B♭/F F C/E Dm7 G7 B♭ F
here to stay, oh I be - lieve in yes - ter - day.
o - ver me, oh yes - ter - day came sud - den - ly.
G/A A7 Dm C B♭maj7 Dm/A Gm C7
3fr
Why she had to go I don't know, she would - n't say.
G/A A7
I said
Dm C B♭maj7 Dm/A Gm C7 F
some - thing wrong, now I long for yes - ter - day.

Em
A7
Yes - ter - day, love was such an eas - y
Dm
Dm/C
B♭
C
game to play. Now I need a place to
B♭/F
F
C/E
Dm7
G7
B♭
F
hide a - way, oh I be - lieve in yes - ter - day.
F/C
G/B
B♭
F
Mm mm mm mm mm mm mm.
rit.